DADSHIP
&
DISCIPLESHIP

David E. Schroeder is president of Nyack College. He earned an Ed.D. in religious education and is founder of Master-Works (http://www.gospelcom.net/mw/), an interdenominational organization committed to helping local churches disciple men. His other books include *Follow Me: The Master's Plan for Men* and *The Broken God: Power under Control.* David and his wife, Betzi, have three grown children.

DADSHIP & DISCIPLESHIP

Character Where It Counts Most

David E. Schroeder

Foreword by Jay Kesler

Baker Books

A Division of Baker Book House Co
Grand Rapids, Michigan 49516

To Christine, Matthew, and Brian,
the three best teachers I have had
in my most important subject: dadship.
You did not choose me, but I chose you.
Remain in my love.

© 1997 by David E. Schroeder

Published by Baker Books
a division of Baker Book House Company
P.O. Box 6287, Grand Rapids, MI 49516-6287

Printed in the United States of America

Library of Congress Cataloging-in-Publication Data

Schroeder, David E., 1946-
    Dadship and discipleship : character where it counts most /
David E. Schroeder ; foreword by Jay Kesler.
        p.   cm.
    Includes bibliographical references.
    ISBN 0-8010-5716-7 (paper)
    1. Fatherhood. 2. Fatherhood—Religious aspects—Christianity. 3.
Fathers. 4. Fathers—Religious aspects—Christianity. 5. Character. I.
Title.
HQ756.S39   1997
306.874'2—dc21   96-45043

For information about academic books, resources for Christian leaders, and all new releases available from Baker Book House, visit our web site:
http://www.bakerbooks.com

Contents

Foreword

Nothing is more clear to me after forty years in youth related ministries than the fact that the confusion around fatherhood and maleness is a central cause of much of our societal malaise. We need clear teaching and encouragement for fathers in all areas of life, perhaps most importantly in the church. This is a book dealing with fatherhood on a most practical level.

God is our Father, and indeed our understanding of the Christian gospel is related directly to the convergence between an earthly experience with our fathers and the biblical narrative. Children who have happy and secure relationships with their fathers find the message of Scripture easily within their grasp. Those who have experienced dysfunction of one kind or another struggle with faith until the negative experiences have been reinterpreted through deep reflection on years of alternate experiences. What is at stake is not merely the breakdown of the family but also the gospel message. This is a book about family and about our spiritual lives as well.

David Schroeder has written a book that will help fathers bridge the gap toward the biblical ideal.

Jay Kesler

Preface

Some of the most influential men in my life have been half-generation men—guys a half generation older or younger than I. These mentors and mentees have had a powerful impact on my life. One of them, Jeff Towers, is eleven years younger than I. He has often heard me tell stories about Chris, Matt, and Brian, my daughter and two sons. Raising his own five children, Jeff is always interested in knowing how things are going for us.

Jeff serves on the MasterWorks board of directors and is very familiar with my other books for men: *"Follow Me": The Master's Plan for Men, The "Follow Me" Manual,* and *The Broken God.* One day, after I had told him one of my most recent escapades with Matt, Jeff said, "You know, maybe your next book should be a down-to-earth look at being a dad, and you could tell some of your stories about your kids." And that was the spark that started this book. Thanks, Jeff.

You may be wondering about the title. Maybe the coined term *dadship* seems a bit cute. My intent, alliteration aside, is to emphasize the relationship between discipleship, which I have written about in my earlier books, and being a dad. I like the term *dadship* because it connotes a status and a function, much like *scholarship* and *leadership.*

Dadship is a tough job; always has been. Today it is even tougher because so many men have been raised with question marks all over their manhood. How can a man be masculine without being macho? How can a dad exert leadership without appearing dominant? Won't being too tender and gentle portray a wrong view of manhood? Questions like these tend to paralyze men who want to be involved actively with their children, or they give excuses to men who are not so inclined. Christian men have the additional complication of many expert voices telling them how to be disciplinarians, how to fill their God-given role as head of the family, and so on. And there is not as much guidance in Scripture as we might like.

I thought it might be helpful for one dad, a very average one, to record some of his struggles, victories, defeats, stories, and inner thoughts through it all. This is definitely not a how-to book. More often it is how not to. My intent is not to extol or recommend my version of dadship, but to help younger dads (I am nearly an empty nester) hear a fresh, firsthand report accompanied by anecdotes and proverbial lessons I have learned, often the hard way. With that understanding and a prayer that God will turn this water into wine to be poured into your new, flexible wineskins, I commit this book to print.

1

Restoring the Hearts of the Fathers

Last words are important. Sometimes death's approach elicits the confession of a crime done years earlier. Or a dying person may reveal the secret location of a treasure. Usually last words are affirmations of love.

Often we remember last words because we know we will never again in this life hear from the dying loved one. When my dad died in 1985, I was at his bedside before he lost consciousness. Knowing his great love for our family over the years, I could tell that his biggest concern was abandoning us, even though my sisters and I were already grown up and married. He did not want my mom to be widowed. Because he was suffering so, I leaned low and whispered to him, "Dad, it's okay for you to die and go to be with the Lord; we'll see you again before too long." After he became unconscious, Mom and I prayed a prayer of release, and soon he was gone.

Last words are uttered not only by the dying. I can remember my last words to my dad but not his last words to me.

Last Words in the Old Testament

If you knew that you were not going to say one more word for forty years, what would your last sentence be? Probably, if you have children, you would leave some parting words of wisdom to encourage them to live by the values most dear to you. In the days of the prophet Malachi, God spoke his last words for four hundred years. What did he say to encourage his children?

His words are recorded in Malachi 4:5–6: "See, I will send you the prophet Elijah before that great and dreadful day of the LORD comes. He will turn the hearts of the fathers to their children, and the hearts of the children to their fathers; or else I will come and strike the land with a curse."

That's it! No "Good-bye," no "Best wishes" or "Good luck," not even an "I love you." Wasn't that a strange way to sign off for four centuries!

Maybe not. When God had Malachi write those words, it was a time of national apostasy. After two exiles and the destruction of Jerusalem and its magnificent temple, the people in Judah several generations later had become bored with their religion. They had lost all reverence for God and respect for his ways. The distinction between right and wrong was blurred. The people sacrificed blind and crippled animals. The priests disregarded the covenant and taught falsehood. Men divorced their wives and married pagan women. Sorcerers, adulterers, and perjurers were tolerated. People gave up all efforts to serve the Lord.

Jewish religion declined rapidly, and as it declined, the moral fabric of the nation wore away. Families were torn apart, and fathers were largely responsible for the moral mess because they were not setting examples or teaching their children to walk in the Lord's ways. Children naturally became disobedient and rebellious.

God's first institution—the family—was caving in. All other institutions stand on the foundation of the family. Family, religion or church, and then national government is the order of priority set by God. The nation cannot be strong for long without a strong church; the church cannot be strong without strong families. Someone has said it this way: America is no stronger than its churches, the churches are no stronger than their families, and the families are no stronger than the fathers.

That's a lot of responsibility to put on fathers. But God put it there. That's why his last word to the people of Israel in the fifth century B.C. was a word of hope. The next time he visited them would be in the person of Elijah, to restore the hearts of the fathers to their children and the hearts of the children to their fathers. It was also a message of dire warning. If God's people would not respond to Elijah, God would usher in the dreadful day of the Lord and strike the land with a curse.

America is no stronger than its churches, the churches are no stronger than their families, and the families are no stronger than the fathers.

Israel needed national revival. Nothing short of that could rescue the nation from doom. Only revival could reconcile fathers with their children, or perhaps, only the reconciliation between fathers and their children could bring about revival.

Moral Decay in America

America is just as desperate for revival today. It's no secret that youthful rebellion against authority, especially parents, is epidemic. Family breakdown due to divorce, abandonment, domestic violence, and verbal, physical, and sexual abuse is now the norm rather than the exception. Qualities such as reverence, respect, and righteousness are nearly unheard of today; these words are hardly in our vocabulary anymore. The outpouring of hatred, anger, and bitterness by today's teens against their fathers is volcanic. And the harvest of hatred we are now seeing may be preferable to the harvest of apathy we are sowing and will reap with the millennium generation now being born.

Several years ago I received a call from a pastor who wanted my help in finding Christian homes for seven children from one family. One of these kids had been molested by her father—with the consent of the mother—and a social agency was seeking foster parents for all seven. We were able to find homes for six of them, but no one would take the biggest challenge, a spunky eight-year-old named Chelsia. Third oldest, she had learned to stand up to her parents in the spirit and language of a drill sergeant. She terrorized everyone.

My wife, Betzi, and I looked deep inside our souls and decided that all our outrage about abortion was hypocritical if we were unwilling to be part of the solution when an opportunity presented itself, or in this case, herself. Opposition to abortion is best expressed by caring for unwanted children. So off we went to pick up Chelsia, encouraged by our sense of righteous fortitude. Little did we know what the next eighteen months would be like, but we got an early idea when she flashed angry eyes at us and would not let either of us touch her as we tried to befriend her. All the way home in the car she wept with an almost inhuman moan.

For weeks every effort to be nice to her resulted in her cursing, crying, or dashing away. Nighttimes were nightmarish for her. Screaming and moaning in her sleep, once she got to sleep, were frequent. We had on our hands an eight-year-old sociopath. Over the next year and a half we saw remarkable progress as the power of unconditional love gradually melted her icy soul.

I went to court with Chelsia when she testified about her father's abuse of her sister. The three oldest—all girls—had to appear one by one, sit in the witness box alone with their father glaring at them, and tell their stories. Everything imaginable came out. Chelsia had told us about some of it—pornographic videos every night, her father coming into her sister's bed frequently, whippings with metal clothes hangers, and worse—but then we learned that the older sister was not the only victim of the sexual abuse. Even the baby boys had been abused by their pedophiliac father.

Justice was served. The father was incarcerated, and the children were removed from the parents permanently. But how can the wounds of such vicious parental abuse be healed? Even with all the best spiritual counsel and psychotherapy available, these children will carry lifelong emotional scars because the person most significant in their lives violated their trust.

Dadship

Words such as *citizenship, stewardship,* and *discipleship* convey the proper performance or execution of the duties associated with the status of citizen, steward, or disciple. Properly performing as a dad has enormous consequences not only for children, but also for society and all its subsets, including schools, churches, and communities. It can be well argued that a father is the most significant person to the development of a person's self-image.

Proper performance as a dad is an intensely spiritual function. The perfect dadship of God indicates that to us. His unconditional love, his limitless grace, his persistent mercy, his abundant provision, his tender communication, his gentle strength, his saving protection, his ceaseless presence, his infinite wisdom, his supreme goodness, his selfless sacrifice, and his eternal reward are but a few of the ways God performs as a perfect Father.

In today's concern for gender-neutral language and political correctness, the masculine identity of God as revealed in Scripture is repeatedly assailed. Despite what anyone thinks ought to be the case, one fact is undeniably true—the Old Testament and New Testament books use masculine terminology to communicate the primary relation of God as Father to his children. Some might say that God is masculine in gender. I do not think Scripture indicates that God is a sexual being in the sense that creatures are sexual beings. But the masculine imagery and terminology are every bit as inspired by God as the rest of Scripture. He who is the sole source of both men and women chose to reveal himself with a masculine identity.

Certainly God relates to us in ways that are sometimes considered strengths of the feminine gender—he nurtures, cares, and shows compassion. But the masculine qualities of God are also evident—he provides, protects, and leads. We must assume that by choosing masculine identity, God wants his children to relate to him in a certain way and wants them to know how to expect him to relate to them. As a consequence, we have a perfect model of the qualities of fatherhood, or dadship.

Elijah Returned

Jews and Christians alike interpret the Malachi passage to refer to Elijah's return before the coming of Messiah. Jesus also understood it that way. During his transfiguration, which was witnessed by three of the apostles (see Matt. 17:10–13), Elijah and Moses appeared and spoke with him. The apostles were overwhelmed by this experience, and it set their minds awhirl. Was this the return of Elijah promised in Malachi? Diplomatically, they broached the subject, and then Jesus surprised them by saying Elijah had already come in the person of John the Baptist.

Jesus was not the only one to know that John was the anticipated Elijah. The angel had announced to Zechariah, John's father, "Many of the people of Israel will he bring back to the Lord their God. And he will go on before the Lord, in the spirit and power of Elijah, *to turn the hearts of the fathers to their children* and the disobedient to the wisdom of the righteous—to make ready a people prepared for the Lord" (Luke 1:16–17, my emphasis). The angel quoted directly from Malachi 4:6 to identify John as the Elijah who was prophesied to return for this powerful family ministry.

A DADSHIP DARE

I challenge you to do something about your dadship. A Dadship Dare, at the end of each chapter, will push you out of your comfort zone a bit so you can grow.

If you could plan your last words, to whom would they be said, and what would you say?

2

A Father's Pride

If ever a dad had a right to be excited about his newborn son, it was Zechariah, for several reasons. First, he and his wife, Elizabeth, are described as being "well along in years," so no doubt he was a proud papa, able to boast about his manly productivity even in advanced years.

Second, an angel had said about the baby boy: He will be great in the sight of the Lord; he will go in the spirit and power of Elijah; he will prepare the people for the coming of the Messiah; he will have a special diet, and so on. Although Zechariah was thrilled, he began to doubt—so the angel shut him up till baby John was born. As soon as Zechariah's tongue was loosed, he began to praise God about the baby. As we read Luke 1:76–79, we're glad he was praising God; otherwise he would sound like a typical bragging papa.

Third, Zechariah was thrilled because as an elder citizen of Israel, he knew how desperately the nation needed the ministry that John would bring to fathers. The angel said that John would fulfill the promise of Malachi 4:5–6. He would "turn the hearts of the fathers to their children and the disobedient to the wisdom of the righteous—to make ready a people prepared for the Lord" (Luke 1:17).

As we ponder John's ministry, we wonder whether he fulfilled the fathers to children part. We know he was the forerunner of Jesus, and we know he lived an ascetic life in the wilderness, and we know he was uncompromising in his call to the Jewish people to repent and be baptized. Where do we see his special ministry to families? John the Baptist did three things that greatly influenced the dadshipping of those who heard him. He preached repentance, he pointed to Jesus, and he provided a role model.

John Preached Repentance

By preaching repentance John called the people to practical lifestyle changes. He wasn't content with an emotional response at the altar. He demanded a 180-degree turnaround in behavior, a transformation of the mind—*repentance.*

Furthermore, he paid a steep price for holding high the biblical standard of purity in family life. King Herod cheated on his wife and his brother by marrying his sister-in-law, Herodias. John took Herod to task for setting such a sinful example. Herod knew John was right, but on his birthday, he was pressured into executing John. Herodias's daughter danced before Herod and his friends. She so pleased Herod with her dancing that he offered her anything she would ask. Her mother made the choice: John's head on a platter. A dysfunctional family was the death of John the Baptist.

As far as we know, Herod never repented. He lost a lot more than his head; he lost his soul. John declares the beginning point for any man who would be a good dad: Repent. We need to change our minds and hearts about who we are and about our dadship. The character qualities needed for good dadship do not come naturally. They come as we submit our wills to God. To do that, we need to deal with the sin in our lives.

Repenting is a good starting point for another reason. We all know about male pride. We know about it because we see it in ourselves. Pride is the illusion of power and of self-sufficiency. We like to think that we are in control. When our children become adolescents, we learn differently real fast. Repentance is the first step in acknowledging that we are not self-sufficient. Repenting requires us to humble ourselves. Many men do not become Christians because they do not want to admit they need anything or anybody. Pity their kids, who grow up with a shell of the man. Restoring the hearts of fathers to their children begins with dads who repent.

John Pointed to Jesus

John's primary ministry was not about families. As the forerunner, John was intent on softening the hearts of the Jews to receive their Messiah. The repentance he called for was not merely about reforming their behavior. Many of us have tried to reform. What we resolve on New Year's Day usually ends before the Super Bowl. Christianity does not require us to reform, but to relate; we relate to the one who will reform us. John pointed to him: Messiah Jesus.

Jesus insisted that John baptize him, not because Jesus needed to repent, but in order to identify with the renewal movement in Israel. As Jesus rose out of the Jordan's waters, John and others heard a marvelous statement from above: "You are my Son, whom I love; with you I am well pleased" (Luke 3:22). What wonderful words! How privileged the children who hear their fathers say that! As John pointed to Jesus, he also pointed to the perfect father/child relationship. Those who saw Jesus saw the perfect Son.

There is absolutely nothing more important that a father can do for his son and for his daughter than point them to Jesus. In fact, if a dad does everything else right, but never points his children to Jesus, he fails as a father. If we do not help our children get to know the Father of us all, we are cheating them out of life's best treasure. The Father has clearly said that to get to know him we must come through his Son. There was a popular song called "Teach Your Children Well." The place to start is teaching them to know Jesus.

If a dad does everything else right, but never points his children to Jesus, he fails as a father. If we do not help our children get to know the Father of us all, we are cheating them out of life's best treasure.

During the past few decades, it has been fashionable to frown upon parents influencing their children about religion. So-called enlightened parents have decided to wait till the kids are old enough to decide for themselves. The Millers, who lived in our neighborhood, said that believing a religion is like choosing which car to buy, a matter of personal taste among several equally valid options. Unfortunately, although their children did get their driver's licenses and buy cars, they never did choose a religion.

Jesus is not one of several valid options. He is the only Son of God. His salvation is the only way to the Father. Truly enlightened parents show love for their children by pointing them to Jesus. Rather than choosing between cars, teaching religion is like providing our children with adequate nutrition. We do not let them eat only what they want until they are old enough to decide whether or not to eat a sensible diet. Knowing the importance of eating well and that in their immaturity children would choose only sweets, we make nutrition decisions for them. If this is important with physical food, it is far more important with spiritual food.

Deuteronomy 6:4–8 and 20–25 teach exceptionally important principles about parents' influence on children's religion. John the Baptist had this kind of instruction from his parents year after year. He was very sensitive to the voice of God because, even as a little boy, he had heard the story of God's choosing him for a special purpose. Our children also need to learn early that God loves them and does, indeed, have a wonderful plan for their lives.

John the Role Model of Manliness

A popular TV commercial features Charles Barkley saying, "I'm no role model." I like Sir Charles, but whether he wants it or not, young people watch him, and because they admire his basketball skills he has become a hero to them. Kids aren't sophisticated enough to separate the player from the person. They take him as a whole package.

Every dad is a role model whether he likes it or not. Like Charles, he may be a positive or a negative model, but his influence is inevitable. A dad cannot say, I'll be a good dad, but I don't care about being a good husband. The children will watch him in all his roles.

Although apparently he did not marry, John embodied many exemplary qualities. He was a man of passion. He cared deeply about important things—things like righteousness, fairness, poor people. He was a practical man, very concerned about financial fairness. When people asked what they needed to do to repent, he told them to be generous with others less fortunate. Tax collectors and soldiers were told not to abuse their positions for selfish gain, and well-to-do folks were told to share with the poor (see Luke 3:10–14).

John was manly, not in a showy, macho sort of way, but in a genuine, masculine, confident way. We have already seen how he stood up to Herod. He confronted soldiers and tax collectors. He lived in the desert. Jesus even commented about his fashion: "What did you go out into the desert to see? . . . A man dressed in fine clothes? No, those who wear expensive clothes and indulge in luxury are in palaces" (Luke

7:24–25). In that same speech Jesus declared, "I tell you, among those born of women there is no one greater than John" (v. 28). Jesus surely had a high view of John's manliness.

John was a humble role model. He had a true picture of himself and didn't pretend to be greater than he was. At the peak of his popularity, he deferred to Jesus and told others to follow Jesus. Rather than becoming jealous, John said, "He must become greater; I must become less" (John 3:30).

John was not only humble, he was brutally honest. New Testament scholars are not entirely sure whether John 3:31–36 continues quoting John, but they surely ring true with what we know about him. He honestly declared Jesus' identity and spoke some of the most important words in the Bible in John 3:36: "Whoever believes in the Son has eternal life, but whoever rejects the Son will not see life, for God's wrath remains on him."

John didn't hedge about words. As a realist he knew that the unrepentant are already under God's wrath. Jesus had said the same thing in John 3:18. No man can become the man God intended him to be without submitting to Jesus Christ.

Sometimes we men can be pretty stubborn. We want things to be the way we want them, and we don't want others to limit our options. We wrap our manliness in our freedom. If you try to fence me in, you are playing with my freedom and had better watch out. Maybe that's why we identify so readily with cowboys. They seem so free and independent. The Marlboro man is not only good-looking in a rugged sort of way, but sitting on his horse he has all the options in the world and sings, "There's no place that I'd rather be." But limitations are real. Options are limited. When it comes to dealing with God, he sets the rules. If he says there's only one way, that's it. He doesn't negotiate.

Think of it from his perspective. He had an only beloved Son. Knowing full well the vicious, inhumane treatment his Son would receive, he sent him to earth. Jesus lived a perfect moral life and made the only acceptable sacrifice for sin.

He died an indescribably painful and undeserved death to set us free from the curse of sin. After all that, we come along and say, "Well, that's nice of you, God, but we want more options. One way is not enough."

Suppose you had a son who was in a war. A grenade is thrown into his bunker, and to save the lives of his friends he throws himself on the grenade and is blown to the four winds. One of the spared friends visits you years later, and you invite him for dinner. At the table you say to your visitor, "Before we eat, we always bow our heads for a moment to remember our son." Suppose the one whose life was saved by your son then said, "Not me; I'm not going to do that. How can you insist that I bow my head? I'm a free man. I live the way I want to live. Who cares that your son died?"

What would your response be? You just might not want him to share the meal at your table. You might just want to say, "Now look here, you owe your entire life to him. If you want to be at my table, you're going to have to respect my wishes."

God surely has the right to determine how we come to him. He provided a way; we must either go his way or continue under his wrath.

The starting place for being a good dad, son, or man is allowing God to be your Father, which begins with repentance. And to do that you must accept his Son.

A DADSHIP DARE

Think about your dad for a moment. In what ways was he a good role model for you? Regardless of all else, thank God for that, and if you can, tell your dad you appreciate him for that quality.

3

The Fourth World

Several years ago I received a call from Stan Farmer, who directs His Mansion, a retreat and rehabilitation center in New Hampshire. The young people who go there are struggling with addiction or abuse. Stan and his staff have built a community where these young people find safety and hope. His Mansion is located in a rural area that is ideal for the kind of industry that supports the daily needs of the residents—they grow their own food. I call them Farmer's farmers.

As they work, study, worship, and live together, they gradually begin to experience love—many of them for the first time. Some stay only a few weeks; others stay for more than a year. It's a wonderful ministry, in operation now for over twenty-five years.

Stan called to ask me to speak at the Fourth World Conference, sponsored and hosted by His Mansion. I asked, "What's the significance of the name?" Stan told me that he drew the idea from Acts 1:8, where Jesus told his disciples that they would be witnesses in Jerusalem, Judea, Samaria, and to the uttermost parts of the earth. Then he said, "We always hear about the third world, the undeveloped and unreached uttermost parts of the earth. Many mission groups are focused on reaching the third world. The first world is our immediate neighborhood, America, and the second world is the developed world overseas that has been evangelized."

Untouchables

"So, what's the fourth world?" I asked.

"The Samaritans," Stan told me, "were the forgotten undesirables, the untouchables of society in Jesus' day. In our day they are the abused, abandoned, and addicted young people who live right among us. We shun them and consider them to be only problems we wish would go away."

From traveling in India, I knew exactly what he meant by "untouchables." They are the lowest, most despised class, the ones no one wants anything to do with. "But what's this Fourth World Conference all about?" I asked.

"People who work with these young people, like we do, are scattered all across America," he told me. "We get them together for encouragement and training."

"But why do you want me to come?" I asked. "I don't know much about those kinds of ministries or about those kinds of kids."

Stan told me something I'll never forget. "Dave, I have worked with hundreds of severely troubled kids for over twenty years now, and I've never met one, not one, who had a good experience with his or her dad. A father is the most significant figure in anyone's life, and these kids all hate their fathers."

Very few things I've heard have affected me like that statement. My dad was a great dad, and there was a deep bond between us. I'd never thought about the idea that every kid's dad plays such an important role in his or her life.

Stan continued, "All our work is prescriptive; we treat the kids who come to us bruised and wounded. But knowing of your work with men in MasterWorks, I want you to come with a preventive message. Talk to these youth workers about the character qualities of godly fathering, so they can better counsel the kids."

Iron John

Hearing Stan talk about the responsibilities of dads reminded me of an earlier experience. Several years ago, a men's movement started in the United States. Men in small groups would go to a remote retreat center and do some bizarre things to connect with the little boy or the emerging man within them. Many of them had read Robert Bly's popular book *Iron John,* a modernized tale of an old epic about a young prince and what he had to do to gain independence and self-identity.

Having started MasterWorks in 1986 and being intensely interested in the spiritual maturing of men, I read *Iron John* and tried to follow the developments of the men's movement. From what I can tell, it was like a kerosene fire—a huge blaze that died down quickly.

In 1992 I met Bill McCartney, who was head football coach of the University of Colorado Buffalos. Bill had achieved huge notoriety because his team had won the national championship once and had tied for number one another time. He was in the early stages of launching Promise Keepers when I met him.

He and I chatted for a while and observed that the feminism of the seventies and eighties was a movement for new rights and a celebration of victories (bra burning being its highly evocative symbol). The Christian men's movement is not about rights, but about responsibility. There is little celebration or jubilation in it because men are being sobered up about how badly we have discharged our responsibility to our country, our churches, and our families.

Since then, of course, Promise Keepers has grown enormously and has outlasted the secular men's movement because its message and its purpose are far more significant. In the secular movement, once a guy has gone out into the woods, stripped naked, decorated himself with Indian war paint, whooped around a fire with other guys, and told his deep, dark secrets about feelings of inadequacy, there's not a lot more that can be done. Not so for Christian men. The to-do list of reclaiming spiritual responsibility in the home and in the church will keep many men going and growing for years.

"Many Men Have No Model for Fatherhood" is the title of an article that appeared in the 6 December 1993 edition of my local paper, the *Rockland Journal News*. The article was mostly a discussion about *Man Enough* (New York: Putnam, 1993), a book by Frank Pittman, an Atlanta psychiatrist. Pittman observes that increasing numbers of boys grow to adulthood fatherless due to emotional or physical abandonment. In an age of rising divorce rates, he says, we are seeing the fallout of

> an ill-advised, foolish experiment in seeing whether it was possible to raise boys into manhood without fathers. . . . It was a crazy thing to do. Even the most primitive societies know better. Because boys end up without domestic models of masculinity. They have mythic heroes of overblown masculinity, and they have blood brothers who go through puberty with them, but there's nothing in between. There are boyish guesses at what men are supposed to be. But they don't know what a man's life is like.[1]

Pittman calls this a state of emergency. The article goes on to say,

> With each generation, it gets worse. Children of divorce are much more likely than others to have marriages that end in

divorce, too, and "the sons of men who couldn't make commitments are very much at risk for not being able to make commitments themselves."[2]

They become obsessed with the nearly full-time job of trying to prove their masculinity to themselves and other men, and "never get around to doing what men do. Now, what men do—the most important thing for a man to do in life—is to be a father to his children."[3]

The "mythic heroes of overblown masculinity," as Pittman calls them, are athletes, film warriors, and entertainers. While they may be inadequate role models, many young people worship such figures because of their disdain for the antiheroes they live with, their fathers.

No Substitute for Character

At the Fourth World Conference I listened more than I talked, and I heard some nearly unbelievable stories of the young people these folks were helping or had tried to help. Those attending the conference told me these stories.

Allen, for example, is now middle-aged and produces a television sitcom. On his show, the husband-father is a boorish idiot, a lot like Al Bundy on *Married with Children.* Not so subconsciously, Allen uses his TV production to send a message about his view of fathers. Allen was raised in a fundamentalist religious family. His father, very strict, imposed and enforced legalistic standards on his children. His harsh discipline bordered on violence. Let us call Allen's father Authoritarian.

Allen grew up suppressing bitterness toward his dad and hatred for his church. After he was kicked out of a conservative Christian college for showing up drunk at a chapel service, Allen transferred to a city college and majored in performing arts. At that point he rejected his father's guidance and alienated him. As Allen's career progressed, he suffered bitter memories of the father who cared more for rules than for a relationship with his son.

Authoritarian would have been a better dad if he had learned to exercise **flexibility.** So many conservative Christian parents drive their teens away because of inflexibility. Their kids are never free to be children. The religious rules reign in the home. These parents are like the Pharisees; they prefer the old wineskins to the wine itself, as Jesus talked about in Luke 5:37. Well-adjusted teenagers have flexible folks.

Brenda was a young, runaway dropout, deeply addicted to hard drugs. After escaping her suburban home, she migrated from family to family among her close friends. Some of them shared drugs with her; others tried to get her to quit. All of them sympathized with her leaving home.

Brenda's father was Absentee. He was a high-powered, workaholic perfectionist. Although in her early years Brenda showed great promise as a gymnast, she was never commended by her father. In fact, he never saw her perform. He always had more important things to do trying to climb the corporate ladder. Her mother died from cancer when Brenda was nine; Brenda was left virtually on her own. Rather than filling the gap left by the lost mother, Absentee devoted himself all the more to his career. Within a few years Brenda began to use a needle to deal with her pain. At times she left obvious clues about her drug use, hoping her father would notice and come to her aid. If he noticed, he didn't seem to care. So she split.

The character quality of **selflessness,** which Jesus discussed in Luke 9:23–25, was sorely missing in Absentee. His life was totally absorbed in furthering his career, and Brenda just couldn't help him much with that. Self-centered ambition and selfish living have alienated many parents from their children.

32

When he was around, Alcoholic, Cedric's father, was always drunk. But he was less violent then, so Cedric didn't mind. Cedric received the fatherly attention he craved at age five from his uncle. As he and his uncle grew closer, some strange things began to happen to him. Later he learned that his uncle was sexually molesting him. He longed for the male attention; still, he wished for his dad's love rather than his uncle's interest.

His uncle moved away. There were no other significant men in his life. When his sex hormones began to function at adolescence, it seemed natural to look to other men to fulfill his desires. Cedric finally found his way to His Mansion, where he received Christian love and teaching. He hopes that by God's power he will refrain from further homosexual behavior. Sometimes he dares to hope that God's power could help his father, too.

Alcoholic sorely lacked **integrity.** He was like the hypocrite Jesus mentioned in Luke 6:39, the blind trying to lead the blind. While he romanced his bottle of booze, his son was romanced by a pedophile. Lack of character in one generation almost always results in serious problems in the next.

As a straight-A student in high school, Daphne received an academic scholarship to an exclusive college for women. She couldn't get away from home fast enough. She couldn't understand how her mother could tolerate Adulterous, her father. This man lived shamelessly in an affair with a woman from his workplace, and she wasn't the first one. He would brag about how good he was in bed with her and compare his wife to her. Pornographic magazines littered any rooms of the house he used, and often he brought home X-rated videos.

Daphne hated him. He made lewd comments about her body. In her early teen years he seemed always to be trying to get her to sit on his lap. When she caught on to his lechery, she resisted him strongly.

33

In college she began to explore her sexuality with other young women. She didn't think of herself as a lesbian, but her hatred for her father seemed to affect her attitude toward all men. Daphne liked the sensitivity and gentleness she found among women and gradually got closer to a friend who seemed to long for the same intimacy. She enjoyed her father's disgusted sneer when she told him about her lover.

Her father's adultery and shameless carnality revealed a very shallow character. No one held him **accountable** for indulging his fleshly appetites. He was in great spiritual jeopardy, if we understand Luke 17:1–3, because not only was he guilty of great sin himself, but he caused "one of these little ones" to sin.

Erica ran away from the country. Unfortunately, her rural upbringing did not spare her from a brutal life. Her father was a hardworking farmer who seemed to need to project a macho, materialistic image. She thought he was ashamed of his profession and worked hard to compensate. While he provided for them, he was also very violent with his family. He often used electric cords to beat Erica and her brothers, nor was her mother spared. Many mornings Erica saw bruises and welts on her mother's face and arms.

To escape Abusive, Erica, at age fifteen, headed for the largest city in her state. Her plan was to get a job as a waitress. She could earn the best money as a barmaid. She lied about her age, and before long she was serving her customers more than drinks; the money was good, so why not? Within a year she had a manager (that is, pimp) who took good care of her and brought her many more customers. Another prostitute once told her that female prostitutes hate men. She did not have a difficult time believing that.

Abusive lacked **trustworthiness.** The parable in Luke 16:1–13 tells about the stewardship of relationships. Erica's father's brutal violence against his own wife and children set him apart as a monster. Totally lacking in trustworthiness, he violated what should be the natural instinct for males, namely, protecting loved ones.

Finally, I heard about Felix. At age eighteen, by murder, rape, and armed robbery, he rose to warlord of a city gang because of his violent, dominant personality. Everyone feared him; he feared nothing and no one. Several times the police hauled him in for questioning, but he was far too clever to be held.

The only person Felix seemed to care about was his mother. He would do anything for her—except change his ways. His father was Anonymous. Felix had never seen the man. As a little boy he'd asked who his daddy was, but his mother always said his daddy was God and he was a special gift. By the time he became a young man, Felix gave up trying to learn his father's identity. If he ever meets him, Felix wants to kill him.

Anonymous lacked **courage.** When he impregnated Felix's mother, he did not have the courage to marry her and help raise his son. Most likely he went on to new conquests. Perhaps he fathered many more children who never knew their dad. A good dose of the kind of courage Jesus demonstrated in Luke 22:66–70 would help deadbeat fathers fulfill their responsibilities and raise children for God's glory.

The Anger Factor

Allen, Brenda, Cedric, Daphne, Erica, and Felix have one thing in common. Their lives are dominated by anger, anger at their fathers. These six represent millions of Americans, young and old. When you connect the idea that a father is the most significant figure in a person's life to the horrible way the job is being done by so many fathers, you see why so many people are bitterly angry at their fathers.

Anger against fathers may often be justified. But the losers in the deal are the children of these failures as fathers. Dads

are just too significant for us to be unscathed by their pitiful performances. Having a bad father inevitably causes deep
wounds and severe scars.

After I told the story about Felix at a men's seminar, I met
Joe. He said he could identify with Felix. "I have no idea who
my father is. Neither does my mother. But there's not a day
goes by without my thinking about him. He's the most influential person in my life. But I don't think I'd want to kill him
if I knew who he was. I've already forgiven him and my mom.
I sure would like him to be my friend and dad."

**When you connect the idea that a father is the most
significant figure in a person's life to the horrible
way the job is being done by so many fathers, you
see why so many people are bitterly angry at their
fathers.**

Joe is in the fortunate minority; he does not let anger rule
his life because he has learned to forgive. Someone told him
that as long as he harbored resentment against his dad he
would never be free to love God or other people the way he
should. In fact, Joe told me, "I think because God is our heav-
enly Father, our attitude toward our earthly fathers can influence our theology, the way we view God."

If you have a difficult time trusting God, maybe it is because
your father was untrustworthy. If your father was overly strict,
you might view God as unforgiving and stern. A weak or absent
father who made his wife do all the disciplining might be the
reason you view God as remote and uninterested.

An Exhortation

These six fathers surely represent the worst in fathering.
But their children are not the only angry children. Many,

maybe most, young people today do not have positive attitudes toward their fathers. Anger infests them. They may hide it, but a little probing may bring out some serious venom. How can dads do a better job?

Obeying the many biblical principles for godly living will result in our being good people, but Scripture does not give us a lot of guidance for effective parenting. However, some very precise commands for fathers are given: "Fathers, do not exasperate your children; instead, bring them up in the training and instruction of the Lord" (Eph. 6:4), and "Fathers, do not embitter your children, or they will become discouraged" (Col. 3:21).

The Lord knows all about the anger factor; he knows how important dads are to kids. That's why he warned us not to exasperate or embitter our children. Scripture does not allow any excuses for alienating our kids. The unconditional love God demonstrates for us is exactly the kind of love we need to show our kids.

A DADSHIP DARE

What do you think about Stan Farmer's statement, "A father is the most significant figure in anyone's life"? How does that idea relate to Ephesians 6:4 and Colossians 3:21?

4

The Paternal Umbilical Cord

A popular motto says, "Any man can be a father; it takes a special man to be a dad." Fathering a child is a strictly biological act; being a dad is a fully absorbing spiritual activity. People are finally noticing the devastating effects on society and individuals of life without Dad.

Even secular society has seen the bankruptcy of the no-dad fad. Dr. Joyce Brothers recognized the powerful and wonderful effect her father had on her upbringing. In "Is He a Good Dad?" Brothers helps readers begin to answer the title question by asking nine others.

1. Is he there?
2. Is he involved?
3. Does he cheer his kids' successes?
4. Can the kids count on him?
5. Does he tune in to his kids?
6. Is he understanding in a conflict?

7. Does he create magic memories?
8. Does he bring his problems home?
9. Does he back up his wife?[1]

Dr. Brothers also cites research from a variety of sources that demonstrates the following:

> Paternal involvement can be a key factor in a child's development. Four separate studies of children whose fathers were responsible for at least 40 percent of their care found that the youngsters demonstrated better thinking ability, increased empathy for others and a greater ability to rely on their own judgment. . . .
>
> Research has linked father absence to a lower I.Q., poor school performance, delinquency and problems handling aggression. . . .
>
> Henry Biller, co-author of *The Father Factor,* says that children with effective fathers get along better with their peers and display more social confidence. They are more comfortable in new situations, adapt to change more easily and score higher on intelligence tests.[2]
>
> Phyllis Bronstein, an associate professor of clinical psychology at the University of Vermont, says research suggests that fathers are more likely than mothers to teach physical competence, adventurousness, new skills and confidence in asserting opinions.[3]

Whether he is a positive, a negative, or an absent influence in their lives, Father is extremely significant to every son and daughter. I recall the intensity of Joe's statement about his father, whose identity he did not know: "He's still the most influential person in my life." The father bond stays with us through life, for good or ill.

Jerry Johnston has noted, "Research has repeatedly documented that a child who enjoys a positive and continuous relationship with his or her father tends to have a good self-concept, higher self-esteem, higher confidence in personal and social interaction, greater moral maturity, reduced rates of unwed teen pregnancy, greater internal control and higher career aspirations."4

Most Christian fathers will rejoice when reading these findings that confirm what they know instinctively, that the father's role is essential. Yet they may also feel insecure about the heavy responsibility. Indeed, many men cop out of their responsibilities. And the Christian father has a few other important tasks besides those implied in the nine questions asked by Joyce Brothers.

Asking the Experts

Suppose I could really get inside the heads of my three kids, ages 25, 22, and 17, to find out what kind of dad I've been. Talk about scary—maybe even foolish! But I put pen to paper and wrote twenty-two questions that I thought would give me insight into the perspectives Christine, Matthew, and Brian have on my fathering. My purpose was twofold: First, I wanted to open doors to intimate conversation concerning unfinished business. I knew I wasn't an A, and maybe not even a B, dad; C+, I hoped. Some issues these young adults carried needed to be exposed. Second, I was contemplating writing a book, this one. What insights might my kids share that would help other dads? As you read some of their responses, which they were glad to share even for publication, you will see that I did not have to worry about their willingness to be honest, even when it hurt.

1. How would you describe our relationship?
2. Tell me your memories of some of our best times together.
3. What was your favorite vacation or holiday?
4. What have been your favorite gifts?
5. What other story from our lives should I write about?
6. Did you ever see me misbehave toward your mom?
7. What occupation would you want me to have?

8. How has being the oldest/middle/youngest child affected your development?
9. How are you most like me?
10. How do you not want to be like me?
11. When did you feel most misunderstood by me?
12. What unreasonable pressures have I put on you?
13. When were you most angry with me?
14. When were you most afraid of me?
15. What have been your biggest surprises from me?
16. What decisions disappointed you most?
17. What was the most important discussion we had?
18. What event caused our relationship to improve most?
19. If you were my pastor, how would you encourage me to grow?
20. What key episodes in a child's life does a dad need to be sensitive to?
21. What do you need most from me?
22. How can I be a better dad?

One of the things I learned from discussing these questions with Chris, Matt, and Brian is that a child's attachment to his or her father can take several forms. The father bond can offer security, like a bungee; suffocation, like a noose; or guidance, like reins.

Security Cords

In some ways, that father/child bond is a wonderful security. All of us are dropped into this world without our permission or awareness. Our parents are sort of like a bungee cord; we enjoy the security of being held by their protection while we bounce around in the early years. A positive dad is a strong support. His love and trust can help a young person become confident.

While our children were growing up, we lived in eight cities and in fourteen houses. Many child psychologists might expect such mobility to traumatize children. And, to be sure, several times we felt very concerned about how a move would affect one or other of the children at a crucial time of development.

When I asked the kids about which decisions disappointed them most, I expected their answers to focus mostly on moving. Seventeen-year-old Brian said, "During each move, our family came together more as a unit." Matt, twenty-two, started to answer that some of the decisions to move bothered him but then said, "I can't really say I've been real upset about moving." In fact, some of their best memories center around some of the unusual places we've lived. Picnics in the rain in England and motorcycle rides around the Caribbean island of Bonaire every Saturday came to mind for all three kids as special times. The fatherly cord of confident security was a big factor for their positive memories of moving.

Only one move really bothered Chris. We owned a house in a very nice town in New Jersey and kept ownership of it when we moved to England, a move we expected would keep us there for a long time. After two years, it became apparent to our mission leaders that it would be best for us to return to the United States.

Thinking we knew what was best for the kids—without asking them—Betzi and I decided to move back into our house in New Jersey. We thought it would be best for the kids to resettle in the familiar neighborhood and in their old schools. Chris said, "Coming back to New Jersey was a major disappointment for me. I hated living there before we left for England, and when we came back, it was the last place on earth I wanted to be." But Chris has learned to emulate our confidence in making a decision and trusting that, regardless of whether we are 100 percent sure of it, we can weather the consequences of it. When I asked her, How are you most like me? her first idea was confidence. "I tend to go in and do things, like let's go into this situation and make it better."

The security cord also appears in times of adventure. Discussing his favorite vacation, Matt recalled that when he was eight, he and I were climbing a mountain in Switzerland. Having gotten off the main path, we were ascending a bank so steep that we were on hands and knees using the long grass to pull ourselves up. We came upon a hoselike tube sort of buried in the grass, so we pulled ourselves up on it for about thirty yards—until we got to its end and found it was not attached to anything. As it turned out, our confidence was not well placed, but Matt's confidence in me was absolute. Matt recalled the humorous sequel to the story: "At the top we climbed over a rail right into an outdoor restaurant with people looking at us and wondering where we had come from. They were as surprised to see us as we were to see them."

Suffocation Cords

The paternal bond can get a bit tight at times and can begin to suffocate a child. In most two-parent families, one of the parents may be noticeably harsher than the other. When the father is the more stern, a dangerous dynamic is possible. Because of the father's superior size and strength, the young child may easily be intimidated. In our family this was a problem at times, and I was the one least aware of it. I think our kids would say they have always been confident of my love for them. I am liberal with my affection, although that was a learned behavior for me. Hugs, kisses, and lap-sitting have been part of daily life. But the physical affection did not totally offset the feelings of physical intimidation, especially for Chris and Brian. Recalling when they were most afraid of me, they both referred to punishment time.

> CHRIS: I remember when we were little it was always, "Don't do that 'cause Dad will spank us." It was very scary, the anticipation. Once when Matty and I were very little we were run-

ning around the dining room table. Mom told us to stop, but then we forgot and started again, and Matt tripped over a chair leg and hit his head. You came storming into the room saying we shouldn't be doing that because Mom had told us to stop. And you thought I had tripped Matty and I hadn't, but I didn't get a chance to say I didn't, so I got spanked more than Matthew did. And I remember being very upset with you because you didn't listen to what really happened.

Brian recalled one very traumatic incident:

I failed a class and got an E, but I didn't want you to find out so I made the E into a B. You found out, of course, and that was one of the worst days of my life. You punished me with no TV for the next grading period. The discipline didn't bother me as much as your finding out I had failed. I wanted you to think highly of me and failing a class didn't help. That was the time I actually blew up at you; I actually yelled back at you about all your awards, saying I shouldn't be compared with you, and I'm not you.

That experience had been a real breakthrough for Brian. Neither of the older children had shown such "disrespect" to me, and it came as a surprise that Brian would do it. When he saw that I did not lash back, but was gentle with him, he gained new confidence in my love for him. Loving Brian was not easy for me at first. As a baby and toddler he seemed fussy, and as a child he seemed negative and preoccupied with himself. Though he had the most natural athletic talent of the three children, Brian did not relish pain or discomfort, nor did he like to compete. I wanted him to be fun loving and carefree, as Matt was, or aggressive and dominant, as Chris was. When Brian was about ten years old, I had a moment of enlightenment. He was helping me renovate our house, and I was getting impatient because he didn't do things the way I would do them. On the other hand, I had to admit that he had a much more mechanical mind than I did. My *Eureka!* came, I believe, as a word from the Lord to me: "Just love him as he is." Having preached about love many times, I could hear the echo of my own words, Love is a choice, not a feeling; it is an act of the will, not the emotions. So I decided to love Brian. Within a week Betzi noticed a great change in my attitude toward him, and ever since then, loving him has been a delight.

Matt was always easy for me to love because he was so fun loving. Unlike Brian, Matt was impervious to pain. He could sustain almost any hard shot in football. In high school, he was one of the smallest guys on the team; Matt played offensive center, sometimes going up against defensive noseguards twice his weight. Only once did he get injured, and that was on a kickoff. As you might expect, he was not too fearful of my physical punishment. He says, "You were always a lot larger than I was and that's intimidating, but I don't have any real memories of fear." He was most concerned about what I thought of him. He wanted so much to please me.

Fathers can also suffocate their children with unreasonable expectations. Asking, What unreasonable pressures have I put on you? evoked very vivid memories for all three children.

CHRIS: When I was growing up I had a hard time making phone calls, and I remember feeling very pressured at times to make calls I was supposed to make. I remember I was supposed to call Mrs. Fisher about soccer. For some reason I just hated picking up the phone, and I felt unreasonable pressure from you to call her in the next five minutes. I dialed and let it ring once and hung up immediately. Then I called again right away and it was busy because someone had picked up the phone. Then I came down and said, "Oh, the line was busy"—all because I hated making phone calls. There were some pressures that were good and not unreasonable, such as getting in shape for soccer. Let's get out and run; do a little bit more, a little bit more.

MATT: You had a problem with my handwriting for years and years. You said, "If you don't have neat handwriting people will think you're stupid," which I was always afraid of. My friends all had atrocious handwriting. Since I could never quite have good handwriting, I developed my own system of an alphabet. I've got my own way of writing and it's distinct, not neat nor messy; it's just different. You were somewhat unreasonable about that.

BRIAN: Not unreasonable, but at the time I thought they were—the grades I had to get. You were always telling me the grades had to come from me, not because you wanted them, but because I wanted them. At the time that felt like pressure. I didn't believe you; I thought that you wanted the grades so I had to put out for you. That's when I blew up at you. Maybe also during soccer, you were always telling me to be more aggressive. I don't know why I wasn't, I just didn't have it in me. I don't think that was unreasonable, it was just telling me to be my all and put out during the games. But I don't really feel that you have pressured me throughout life.

Guiding Cords

One time, the two older children thought they were alone, but I was watching. They took some forbidden liberties. When I confronted them, Matt confessed that they would never have done it if they had known I was watching. Matt loved animals; a helpful analogy occurred to me. We discussed the difference between a trained lion and a tamed lion. At a circus, the trainer is in control in the cage with his whip and chair because the lions know he will punish them if they get out of line. As long as he is watching, they behave. But are they tamed? If they were, he wouldn't need the whip, and he wouldn't need to watch. Some children, I pointed out, are like trained lions. They can be trusted only when they are being watched. Other children are like tamed lions. They obey whether or not they are being watched. This image really sunk in with the kids and was useful many times.

The best kind of connection between a father and his children is like reins on a tamed and well-trained horse. The better trained a horse becomes, the less pressure a rider needs to put on the reins. In early days, children need a lot of guidance; the reins need to be kept taut. As they get older, a gentle touch will turn them; a quiet word will bring them to a stop. When his children make important life decisions, a

Even now, ten years after my own dad died, his values, lifestyle, wisdom, and persona remain a rich part of who I am.

father's guidance can be crucial. However, many fathers have lost the privilege of being active in their kids' lives by slamming communication doors during their early adolescence. Especially in the teen years of your child's life it is important to know how firmly or loosely to hold the reins. Most Christian dads seem to grip the reins too hard.

Chris and Matt both referred to their young adult years when asked, What was the most important discussion we had?

> CHRIS: There have been so many. I remember when I lived in Berwyn and you guys were out in Colorado. I don't remember what I was going through at the time, but I was very restless and feeling like God was calling me to be a missionary. I discussed it with Mom and asked her to tell you because I didn't know how to tell you. Then you called back. I remember that discussion vividly because you were very supportive and excited that I had made a decision. You were also open and willing to say that if that's not where I ended up going, that's still fine and you would accept whatever I did decide to do. We also discussed my moving to Nyack. That was difficult, but has been very life changing for me and has been more positive than negative. You have always helped me take a step back and think about things. You didn't say,

Well, I think you should do this. You said, Let's think about this; is this the kind of person that you can see yourself in a relationship with; what are his qualities; what are his characteristics; does he hold up to what you want in a person? It really helped me a lot—sitting down and making a list.

MATT: We had some really important discussions about going to college and what I wanted to do with my life and what paths I wanted to take. I thought I was going into med school, so we plotted a course, and that was very important. We also had important talks about what religion is and who God is and who Jesus is. But the most important discussion I've had with you was in our letter conversations the last semester of my senior year in college. You wrote that it might be tough for me to come home and live for a year because I had changed. I said I had worried about it because, although I care for your approval and want you to be proud of me and respect me, I want to be who I am—not who I think you want me to be. And I don't want to have to be you in any way. I want to be accepted for what I've chosen to be. That was very important.

Brian blessed me greatly by affirming our close and open communication when I asked him, How would you describe our relationship?

Right now as a teenager, compared to my friends, it's the best; a lot of my friends aren't very close to their fathers, but because of the way you raised me, I feel I can talk to you on a personal level whenever I need to about subjects that might be difficult. Once I get past the difficult first moment of asking, I can talk to you easily throughout the conversation.

The father bond will never break. Even now, ten years after my own dad died, his values, lifestyle, wisdom, and *persona* remain a rich part of who I am. Occasionally, in the midst of pressure to make a decision, I tell God that he took my dad too soon and that I need him for guidance and wisdom. But then, of course, I go ahead and make a decision, and I realize later it was what Dad would have wanted.

Dadship and Discipleship

No, the bond won't break, but what kind of cord will it be? Will your kids view it as a bungee, as a noose, or as gentle reins?

A DADSHIP DARE

Why not interview your kids? Choose ten or twelve of my questions or make up some of your own. Ask if they'll let you record the answers so you can review them later.

5

Daditudes

Though nearing our twenty-eighth anniversary, Betzi and I sat in the backseat double dating with a couple who have been our friends for years. On a hunch, Bob decided to check out a place where their teenage children were attending a party—one of those events parents secretly dread. The teens say it will be a small, safe, sinless gathering (well, maybe they don't *say* sinless, but they sure imply it), supposedly chaperoned, at a friend's house and all the other kids' parents are letting them go and how can you possibly deny us this fun time and don't you trust us and we thought you wanted us to have a lot of friends, and so on. As Bob entered the house, he discovered that the chaperons were some juniors and seniors from the high school. Some of the goings-on made him want to grab his kids by the ears and drag them home. Not wanting to humiliate them and eager to keep good communication with them, he invented a reason to ask them to come to the porch for a short talk.

What he said we never knew, but clearly he kept the lines open with his kids. Bob seems to know just the right thing to do and the right way to do it in any situation. How did he come by such wisdom?

Is it wisdom? Or is it character? Bob doesn't have crib notes for what to do in every situation. He hasn't planned for every possibility—unlikely when raising teenagers, whose situations more often than not seem to be impossibilities. Bob is able to act out of a lifetime's reservoir of character, of qualities he developed earlier in his life. Now as he raises his teens, investing in those qualities is paying a handsome return.

There are seven character qualities I call "Daditudes," or Dad Beatitudes. These Daditudes will make you a blessing to your children, and they will also make you blessed.

1. Blessed are flexible dads, for they shall enjoy open communication with their children.
2. Blessed are reliable dads, for they shall retain their children's respect.
3. Blessed are trustworthy dads, for their children will have no lack of material, emotional, or spiritual support.
4. Blessed are dads who love unconditionally, for their children will continue to trust them.
5. Blessed are gentle dads, for they are obeying Scripture.
6. Blessed are humble dads, for they will raise children to be spiritually, socially, and morally mature.
7. Blessed are selfless dads, for they just make good dads.

Blessed Are Flexible Dads

The word *flexible* is not in the Bible, but the concept of flexibility surely is. In Luke 5:37–39, Jesus warned his listeners that new wine should not be poured into old wineskins. New wine is dynamic, fermenting, a chemical reaction that causes expansion. A new wineskin, because it's still flexible, will stretch to accommodate the expansion. An old wineskin is already stretched as far as it can stretch. Putting new wine into an old wineskin will cause the skin to burst.

Being a dad requires flexibility. Young people are dynamic and changing; you never know what to expect next from the younger generation or from your own young person. When a dad tries to raise his children according to the style, mores, fads, and cultural forms of his own generation, he will be strongly resisted. How often did you hear one of your parents say—or have you said it to your teenager?—"When I was your age, . . ."? That formula implies that earlier eras are a standard to judge later eras. No doubt every generation feels the same way about its era.

Not everything changes. The Word of God does not change, and where it speaks to moral issues we need to obey. Often, however, we absolutize a scriptural principle by an interpretation that is unnecessary and arbitrary. Then we imbue it with the same authority as Scripture. The Pharisees were experts at doing this, and we have learned well from them. One example is our law of the quiet time. Well-intentioned disciplers have said that part of being a sold-out Christian is having a disciplined quiet time—devotions—every day. Last I checked, there was no verse in the Bible that says this is a must. Is it a good thing to do? Absolutely. Is it the only way to walk with God? Absolutely not. Early Christians did not have Bibles, and most of them couldn't read anyway. Were they able to walk with God? Obviously.

About the time our children reached adolescence we began to give them opportunities to make decisions for themselves after giving them guidelines and encouragement to do what they thought would please Christ. At times they have done things or gone places we didn't approve. But to our knowledge, they have been honest with us. Communication has stayed open.

Some parents are content merely to have a pleasant atmosphere at home, which will last only as long as certain subjects are avoided. Their children know the taboo topics and are smart enough to recognize these domestic land mines. Mention alcohol, for instance, and *Kaboom!*—Dad explodes. Alcohol is never mentioned again, even when son or daughter desperately needs Dad's wise counsel about it.

True communication allows any topic to be discussed openly, calmly, and nonjudgmentally. By the time your kids are teens, they know your values as well as you do; you gain nothing by a melodramatic, shocked response when your teenager mentions a topic on which you have a strong opinion.

When I asked, How would you describe our relationship? Chris and Matt mentioned the communication between us, as had Brian.

> CHRIS: It's a very open relationship where we can talk to each other and discuss a lot of things, and I feel very important because we do talk about a lot of confidential stuff, and you want my opinions about things.

> MATT: Right now, I'd say it's a fairly active and growing relationship; fairly strong, stronger than most between a father and a son. Fairly honest and open. Intelligent, caring, friendly.

Keeping communication open at the deepest level will not happen by accident. I think a dad needs specifically to tell his son or daughter that it is safe to talk about any topic. That approach worked well with Matt, as revealed when I asked him, What event caused our relationship to improve the most?

> Something you said to me a long time ago set up the possibility of a great relationship. You said that no matter what happens, "I want you to always be able to tell me. If you're smoking or drinking or doing drugs or having sex, I want you to be able to tell me that." That always impressed me; I think that's important, and you said you won't get angry unless it's drugs, and then you might get angry. A simple statement like

that showed me what kind of relationship you wanted to have with me.

Blessed Are Reliable Dads

One of the great blessings of the 1990s is Promise Keepers. The growth of this Christian men's movement has caught everyone by surprise, including founder Bill McCartney. Thousands of men fill football stadiums in nearly every region of the country each year to consider their responsibilities as men of God. I think a huge reason for their success is that in the name Promise Keepers they have captured one of the most

Keeping communication open at the deepest level will not happen by accident. I think a dad needs specifically to tell his son or daughter that it is safe to talk about any topic.

important issues of our day. The marriage covenant, spiritual commitments, promises to kids, contracts in business, financial obligations—all kinds of promises reveal whether a man is a person of integrity. Children, especially, need to see that Dad is dependable and reliable. Does he honor his promises? A dad who is reliable and who keeps his word will retain their respect forever. Contrariwise, a dad who, even with the best intentions, repeatedly breaks his promises to his kids will not enjoy their respect. They may forgive him repeatedly, but they will view him as either dishonest or pitiful.

One thing I have learned about making promises to kids is to be very careful. They have a way of making your casual comment into an oral contract. Nothing crushes children's spirits quicker than when Dad lies to them. Kids will always consider a broken promise to be a lie. Why? Because we taught them well. We teach our children to tell the truth. And they expect their teachers to live the lesson.

After so many moves and so many school changes, Brian, in his freshman year, hoped that our move to Colorado would be fairly permanent, at least long enough for him to graduate from high school. I assured him we would be in Colorado for at least five years, which I believed to be true. When I asked, What was your biggest surprise from me? he answered, "Moving here from Colorado was a surprise. You had promised we would be there for five years, but after two years we were moving. That was a big shock." Moving to Nyack proved to be very positive for him, and he says he doesn't hold it against me, even though it was a big surprise.

This incident was one of several times when I have had to seek forgiveness from my children. That is a difficult thing to do for many dads, including me. In our eagerness to be perfect in our kids' eyes, we can't bear the thought of swallowing our pride, admitting we were wrong, and asking forgiveness. I used to try merely apologizing when I blew it, but Betzi and I had taught our kids the difference between apologizing and asking for forgiveness, and now they hold us to that standard. Asking for forgiveness is superior to apologizing because you must take personal responsibility when asking for forgiveness, as opposed to, "I'm sorry if . . ." or "I'm sorry that. . . ." You also clear the slate by getting an answer— "Yes, I forgive you."

Perhaps the most difficult and most important promise to keep is a commitment to do something with our kids. Why is it so easy to let other appointments supersede appointments with our kids? Some kids make other plans when their fathers agree to do something with them simply because they "rely" on Dad to break the commitment. Little did I realize the importance of these kinds of promises when my children were young. I was relieved when Chris cited her memories of best times together this way:

Growing up, you were around a lot, and that was always fun. Best memories were when the whole family was together doing things. I think of the picnics in England and traveling around, climbing up the mountain in Switzerland, going on bike rides in New Hampshire, and Bonaire when we went on motorcycle rides. Even one-on-one times like recently as we've discussed how I can grow and what areas you've seen me grow; where I think my gifts and my talents lie and how I can better develop them; and assessing what's happened in my life from a better perspective, rather than being very subjective.

Blessed Are Trustworthy Dads

Trustworthiness is a close corollary of reliability. Young people need to know their dads are worthy of their confidence. Children by nature are rather insecure creatures. They are born without the ability to care for themselves, and no matter how much attention their parents give them, it doesn't seem to be enough. Parents struggle to get toddlers to do things they are capable of doing for themselves. It's not that children want to remain dependent, but getting their parents to wait on them reassures them of their parents' care and protection. In teen years they continue to test Mom's and Dad's trustworthiness in little ways, except now the needs are not just material, but also emotional and spiritual. One of the big challenges of parenting is giving children more independence while keeping them secure.

Chris revealed a very important insight for dads of daughters when I asked her, What key episodes in a child's life should a dad be sensitive to? Her response demonstrates how critical it is that a girl sees her dad to be someone she can trust with her changing emotions and body during puberty.

> For girls, especially when they hit adolescent age, it can be hard for their dads to know how to respond. I'm amazed that you and I have always been close. I know that other girls say

they hit a certain age, and they still wanted to be daddy's little girl, but they couldn't anymore because they were all grown up, and their dads didn't know how to react. They seemed to lose interest because they didn't know what to talk about or how to show affection anymore. She has different needs. A dad needs to find what's going to be special between him and his daughter. With you and me we've always had time to talk, like when I come and sit on the arm of the chair and we just talk.

Being trusted with the inner thoughts of your adolescent is a valuable treasure, one that is too rare. From the time a young person is thirteen or fourteen, for another ten years or more, a dad may not hear a genuine word from the depths of his child's soul. This occurs all too often because we dads unconsciously set up boundaries for conversation. Our kids stay far away from those boundaries. They don't want an argument they know they won't win, and they really do want our ongoing respect. If revealing some of their inner lives to us jeopardizes that respect, they will choose silence every time. How can we make sure that we don't set up boundaries for conversation? The key is our body language. Kids read adults better than they read their homework. They can tell when we are near the fringes of our tolerance. We must consciously prepare not to show shock or anger.

Matt helped me see the enormity of this issue when he answered the same question, What key episodes in a child's life should a dad be sensitive to?

What kind of identity is your child taking on? What are you teaching your kids, and do you want to be teaching them that? If you project your child ten years into the future, will he or she be Republican or Democrat, conservative or radical, feminist or chauvinist, gun toting or against arms, hippie or acid core? What types are even out there? Fathers don't know where the breakdowns are or what type their children will become. The more you know about your kids, the less potential there is to be shocked when they turn out the way they do. Every child will eventually shock their father.

"Every child will eventually shock their father." Shocked? Don't be. No doubt you shocked your dad at least once. If our kids know they can trust us regardless of anything— dress, language, music, friends, grades, problems—they will stay open to us. That's far more important than yet another line-in-the-sand confrontation and a speech they know before we say it.

Blessed Are Dads Who Love Unconditionally

When Jesus was asked which was the greatest com- mandment, he said, "You shall love the Lord your God with all your heart, and with all your soul, and with all your mind" (Matt. 22:37 NASB). This one is the greatest because by ful- filling it, all the others will be fulfilled as well. The same is true about unconditional love. As we love our children unconditionally, we fulfill all the other requirements for being excellent parents.

All parents love their kids, right? But this love is not always unconditional. Many parents offer an *if* love or a *because* love, a love based on performance or attributes. If you do_____, if you are _____, if you obey _____; because you are _____, because you did _____, you are loved. When parents love this way, their children sense it; the rela- tionship will break down.

Unconditional love, called *agape* in the Greek New Testa- ment, is *in spite of* love. It is not based on performance, attri- butes, potential, or anything else. Unconditional love is just that—unconditional. A child who knows he or she is loved simply because he or she *is* will be secure and will remain in an open, trusting, communicating relationship with Dad and Mom. Despite the many shortcomings of our parenting, I think our kids would give us an A on this one. Maybe that's why they were able to be so candid in the interviews. Chris revealed her confidence in unconditional love when I asked her, What have been your biggest surprises from me?

> Sometimes I'm surprised how laid back and relaxed you are about things, and I guess I'm still learning how you value the person more than what we do. You want us to act right but you're going to keep on loving us even when we're not totally good.

What if a dad doesn't have unconditional love for a son or daughter? Is it possible to get it? The good news is yes! Agape love comes from the will, not the emotions. If love were only an emotion, God could not command it; because love is volitional, we can develop it. Unconditional love for your kids develops from humility. Every individual is of equal value; you are no better than your kids. Maybe you do some things better than they do; they also do some things better than you do. *Doing* is not the point; *being* is. In God's sight your kids are worth as much as you are, just as they are, without having to change one bit. Keep reminding yourself of this concept until you find yourself loving your kids, in spite of _____.

I am amazed at how sensitive children are to the subtle differences between conditional and unconditional love. If we have hidden agendas for them, if they think they have to succeed at those agendas in order to be loved, they know it to the core of their souls. Matt caught me off guard with his answer to the question, What do you need most from me?

> Nonjudgment. No matter what I do. I've learned that people are fairly proud of themselves. They pretty much like themselves. What some people might think is stupid, I might think I'm doing rather well, and I'd like nonjudgment. I'm not better than you, and you're not better than me. I think that's important—the second part of it—you're not better than me. That's important to remember, no matter what relationship we're talking about.

As I consider reasons why I might judge my kids, I realize I might withhold unconditional love from them because I fear not being unconditionally accepted by my peers, who might judge my parenting. A parent needs to say, Who cares what anyone else thinks? My relationship with my child is far too important to be muddled up by some paranoiac need to be admired by the rest of the world.

Kids can tell when we are more concerned about the impression we make than we are about them. One of the most bonding events in your life with your son or daughter may be a time when you throw reputation and appearance to the wind simply to express your deep love. At age six Chris broke the femur of her right leg, which required her to be hospitalized for a few weeks. As an ambitious pastor, I could ill afford to miss the many evening meetings of a busy church. Little did I know that the investment of those evenings was so important, as Chris mentioned when I asked, What event caused our relationship to improve most?

> When I broke my leg, I remember you coming to the hospital at night and sitting with me. You would watch baseball on TV as I fell asleep, and I knew that you were in the room. That is a warm memory. And then we went to Radio City Music Hall, and I was up on your shoulder. You carried me like a rifle. I was scared up there because the cast was very awkward, but I remember you holding me and I was secure.

Looking back on it, I came to see that as Chris's leg mended, so did our relationship. I had been so intense in pursuing my ministry that she was going to be its sacrificial lamb. One of the conditions that we dare not put on our kids is, "I will love you as long as I can also achieve my other goals." I would rather fail at all my jobs and succeed as a dad than achieve my highest career goal and fail as a dad. Too many kids have been sacrificed to ambition by dads who think the business world or the ministry needs them.

Blessed are the children whose dads demonstrate flexibility, reliability, trustworthiness, and unconditional love, the first four Daditudes.

A DADSHIP DARE

Which of the first four Daditudes do you need to work on most? Why not ask your wife or kids? Next, what will you do about it?

6

Manly Meekness

"If being a good husband and father is so important, and I know it is, why didn't Jesus say much about family life?" This question caught me off guard as I was trying to handle a question-and-answer session during a men's retreat. It surprised me, not because I hadn't made the same observation, but since 1986, when I began ministering especially to men, no one else had ever raised the point. When I wrote *"Follow Me": The Master's Plan for Men,* I had to deal with this anomaly. Why did Jesus skip such a crucial subject? He said more about being a success in business than about being a father. Wasn't family life important in the first century?

Several ideas came to mind as I pondered the question. First, family life was important then, very important; in fact, it was so important that the domestic problems we commonly face were nearly unheard of in that culture. Jewish parents were loving and caring, teenagers did not seem to have their own subculture, families worked together with plenty of quality and quantity time, and extended families gave a wonderful security to the children. At age twelve, Jesus was not missed by Joseph and Mary as they began their trip home from Jerusalem; they assumed he was with cousins, grandparents, or other family members.

But keeping in mind John's mission to restore the hearts of the fathers to the children and the children to the fathers, we know the situation was not perfect. So, again, why did Jesus not speak more directly on the topic of being a good father? I believe the main reason is that Jesus wanted men to become righteous men and to build into their lives the character qualities of the kingdom. Good fathering would be a by-product of kingdom living. A huge portion of his teaching concerns character development. That is the primary thrust of *"Follow Me."* In it we examine fifteen passages in Luke and discover that each time Jesus spoke about discipleship he taught another character quality. For example, the first five are teachability, flexibility, humility, compassion, and integrity. Jesus knew that if men would repent—the first part of his message—and begin to live by his teachings, they would be great dads. The Daditudes we are considering are qualities that are supported by hundreds of verses, and men are to live out these qualities not just to be good fathers, but to be godly men.

Blessed Are Gentle Dads

The apostle Paul was quite specific about the way to be a good father. He told the Ephesians not to exasperate their children (Eph. 6:4), not to provoke them to anger (NASB), but to bring them up in the training and instruction of the Lord. He told the Colossian dads not to embitter their children because they would become discouraged (Col. 3:21). *Gentleness* is the best one-word summary of these two admonitions that are as needed today as they were then. You won't talk with teenagers very long before realizing we have a generation of young people exasperated and embittered toward their fathers. Dads are often harsh, dictatorial, and dominating. Why is this so? Perhaps we have not understood or obeyed the rest of Ephesians 6:4: "Bring them up in the training (discipline, NASB) and instruction of the Lord." Interpreting this passage, John Calvin said, "Let them be fondly cherished . . . , deal with them gently."[1] The words *training* and *instruction* mean nourishing and correction; they emphasize the need for balance between encouragement and rebuke. The goal of mental and moral education is that children will submit to the authority of Christ.

Matt pulled no punches when I asked him, When did you feel most misunderstood by me? He replied, "I can't think of any particular time, but I know events did occur. You had a very overdominant, dogmatic spirit."

Some men might be gentle by nature, but not many I know. We seem to wear our authority right on our chests and to view any challenge to that authority as a challenge to our manhood. How can we be so insecure? Here is this precious little four-year-old girl sitting across the table dawdling with her oatmeal. She's not hungry, doesn't really like eating wallpaper paste with brown sugar, and is eager to watch *Sesame Street*. But as The Father you come down on her like she was public enemy number one. As though she had personally offended you out of blatant rebellion, you bellow something like, "Young lady, you're going to sit there until you have swallowed the last spoonful of that delicious oatmeal, and don't you dare put that spoon down until you are finished!"

Or your seven-year-old boy comes home from school with a note about a PTA meeting. Somehow the note got crumpled and a tad dirty. You lost a client at work that day and your boss was less than pleased. Opening the PTA note, you vent your day's frustrations on the little lad, "Young man, is this the way this note looked when your teacher gave it to you? What did you do, take it to a tractor pull? Why are you always so messy? Can't we just once get a nice clean, unwrinkled note from school? And this is the same way you treat your schoolwork. Doesn't your teacher ever complain about your messy work? When I was a boy . . . blah, blah, blah." Your son tuned you out right after "Young man."

Now your four- and seven-year-olds are fourteen and seventeen, exasperated and embittered. Maybe it isn't like this in your home, but it is in thousands of American homes, Christian and non-Christian. Occasionally the kids may see Dad being gentle, but not consistently. For most men, the words *manly* and *meekness* are contradictory and incongruous.

Meekness is not weakness. Meekness is not weakness. Shall I say it again? You get the idea. The Greek word for "meek" or "gentle" was also used to describe a powerful, wild animal that had been tamed and trained for domestic usefulness. When, for example, a water buffalo has been domesticated, is it any less strong? Of course not. The difference is that now its power is controlled for constructive purposes. This machismo, this sense of power or strength so many men buy into is an exaggeration, a caricature of manliness. A truly strong, secure man does not need to impress anyone. He is quite content to be seen as meek. Only the insecure need to put on the macho act.

How can dads learn to be gentle with their kids? Here are a few practical ideas. First, never punish your children. That's right, don't punish them. Discipline them. There's a big difference. Punishment is retribution, getting back at them. It focuses on the past and is exercised for your benefit, not theirs. Discipline is correction for the future and focuses on the welfare of the child. The motivation is not retribution, but redirection. Youth counselor Bill Gothard gives several principles for effective disciplining. Every step is consciously prochild. When we were young parents, Betzi and I came across these principles; they made a huge difference in the way we disciplined Chris, Matt, and Brian. For example, don't send your kids to their rooms, isolating them from the rest of the family, when they misbehave. Deal with the issue and then reassure them of your love. Sending them away only widens the alienation gap; it sends the signal, "You are disgusting; we reject you." Regardless of what your children may have done, they need to know that while you reject their behavior, you still cherish them.

Also, never show anger. We do not realize how powerful and intimidating we appear to our children. When we express anger at them, they see us as out of control and very dangerous. It may be impossible never to be angry, but anger begets anger, and Paul said do not provoke your children to anger. Shouting ought to be ruled out altogether.

Be accountable to your wife. Tell her she has the right to give you feedback on how you are coming across to the kids. She has a built-in protection mechanism for her kids, and she will be sensitive to their feelings. Be humble enough and smart enough to learn from her.

Play with your kids. This may not seem profound, but your kids need to see you as their friend. When they see you rolling on the floor, playing with Lego blocks, putting together puzzles with them, and just being goofy, then they accept you as a friend. Even when your kids are older they will continue to value your friendship in doing things with them. Chris was thoroughly thrilled when I went to her apartment recently to help with her wedding invitations.

Above all, picture in your mind Jesus as he is described in Matthew 19:13–15, the most powerful man in the world gently loving children.

Blessed Are Humble Dads

Humility is an important spiritual quality, but what makes it especially important for dads? Most men I know do not wrap up their ego needs in their fathering. Most of us get our strokes from success in our careers or through some special ability or achievement. Children pick up on this easily. They discern what is truly important to us. They may get the impression that the little people are not really a major ingredient in the mix of our lives. Many dads are either occupied or preoccupied. Occupied dads are literally not available because of travel, divorce or separation, or a late work shift. Preoccupied dads could be more available but in their scale of priorities, the kids are somewhere in the middle of the list, somewhere after the really significant things in their lives. Kids are important enough to deserve a lot of Mom's time, which must not be quite as valuable as Dad's time, but they have to fit in with the rest of Dad's important schedule.

Many dads are either occupied or preoccupied. Occupied dads are literally not available because of travel, divorce or separation, or a late work shift. Preoccupied dads could be more available but in their scale of priorities, the kids are somewhere in the middle of the list, somewhere after the really significant things in their lives.

Humility calls a dad "not to think more highly of himself than he ought to think" (Rom. 12:3 NASB). Having a realistic appraisal of who we are and of the value of our children is the starting point of humility. If you want some shock therapy to help you gain that realism, try asking your kids, as I asked mine, How do you not want to be like me?

CHRIS: I hope I'm not quite as intense as you are. And you use your intuition on certain things, and sometimes I think you're wrong when you don't think you're wrong. You tend to always be right. You cannot lose in a conversation, and sometimes I wish you hadn't majored in philosophy because you are very good at arguing. You can't even lose a card game without saying that it was luck, and I don't want to be like that, but I sometimes am like that. I don't want to be so caught up in the competition, but rather in the relationship-building.

MATT: I don't ever want to say "I know" to anything. I'm not saying that you are overconfident, but I want to be confident enough to disagree with someone else and have a spirit that doesn't fight the other opinion. That's something I'm dealing with right now, trying to be my own person instead of who I think you want me to be or who I think you are.

BRIAN: To be honest, I can't think of anything. I like the way I've turned out so far. The thing about New Jersey that I remember most is that you traveled a lot, and I would always get sick a day or two after you left, for no apparent reason. I think it would be good to be there more.

I'm still trying to get over those answers. I think they were as surprised that I asked them such a question as I was about their answers. After age nine or ten, when parents are no longer the primary ones whose opinions matter to them (replaced by those odious creatures called peers), your children may have the courage to be honest if you ask them this question.

One important and humbling task is what I call the Puberty Trip. About the time the sap begins to rise in your kids, sometime between ten and twelve for girls and twelve and fourteen for boys, the greatest thing you can do is to go on a special outing, just you and your daughter or son. The agenda? Talk. Talk about the things that matter most to you. Talk about the things that matter most to your child. Most likely they will be similar topics: how to relate to the opposite sex, what values are foundational for making decisions, how you can keep communication open between you during the teen years, what your child can expect to have happen to his or her changing body, and so forth.

Puberty is the springtime of life. It's when the glands take over. It's the dawning of adolescence. I think it calls for extra dadship efforts. For each of my boys I set aside several days to go away to do something fun together and have some serious discussion.

Matt and I went to New Hampshire to help renovate a house. He enjoyed being trusted with tools, and as we were laying carpet, some deep stuff came out about how he viewed himself. Brian and I spent a week at a farm in Minnesota. I taught him how to use a rifle, and then after a few days I let him take it into the woods for target practice. Being trusted like that meant a lot to him. The value of being with me was very different for each of them. For Matt it meant deep conversation and learning that I could be his pal. For Brian it meant I loved him as much as Matt and that I would trust him with the gun. Looking back, I probably should have spent such a time with Chris, but she and I always had an easy time of communicating deeply, and I thought her mom could contribute more to her puberty onset than I.

By puberty most kids already know more about the birds and the bees than the birds and the bees know. Much of their information has come from value-free sex education classes and from kid talk. This is a good time to make sure they view sex in the context of biblical values. It's also a time to talk about career choices, spiritual disciplines, sibling relationships, their hopes and dreams, their fears and failures, and their special gifts from God.

Some kids will take to this like fish to water; others, like fish to mountain climbing. Be careful in the approach. I took my nephew Aaron on such an outing. Because we didn't know each other too well, I invented a game in the car as we traveled to the cabin. "Let's take turns asking each other questions," I said, "but each of us is free to pass if he doesn't want to answer one." Aaron liked that idea; it opened conversation that got progressively deeper throughout the weekend.

Several no-no's about the puberty trip. Do not take anything that hints of your work. For example, briefcase, cellular phone or beeper, "catch-up" reading material, or your Day-Timer. Also, do not turn conversations into lectures. Do not use yourself as the model for your child's behavior. Do not plan so much activity that you have no opportunity for serious, private conversation. An effective puberty trip is one where your son or daughter knows you are there 100 percent for him or her, and that all of his or her important topics have been discussed openly.

One of the most important topics is dating. It has been my practice to ask my children to assess their boyfriends or girlfriends on the basis of character, intellectual compatibility, and physical attractiveness. At first they had a difficult time knowing how to quantify such attributes, so I resorted to the old rating system using a one-to-ten scale. When Chris told me she was going out with a guy, I would say, "One-to-ten on the three." She would then assess him: "Character eight, intelligence six, and appearance nine," or something like that. The value of this little exercise is fourfold: it tells your children you are interested in knowing about every person they date; it encourages them not to go out with people simply for something to do or because they are asked; it helps you communicate an important priority of values; it lets them know that you believe every date is a potential mate.

This last idea, every date is a potential mate, has received quite a bit of discussion in our home and others. Can't you just hear your beautiful young daughter pleading, "But, Dad, I'm not going to marry him." My reply to Chris was: "Okay, so tell me before your first date with the guy you're going to marry that he's the one! It doesn't work that way. When I first asked your mom out, I had sworn off girls for a year; I surely didn't intend anything serious. You never know what the chemistry and romantic magic will do, so you better make sure each guy you date rates high in the essentials."

Humility will enable a dad to see that discussions like these may be the most important things he will ever do, and that includes his career. Humble dads will harvest maturity in their kids. Spending time talking about the important things of life will give your kids spiritual, social, and moral maturity far beyond their peers. If you are concerned about the impact of negative peer pressure on your children, these important dad and daughter and dad and son discussions are the best defense you have.

Blessed Are Selfless Dads

Selflessness is a cumbersome word, but it best conveys a very important concept. Selflessness places a high priority on your children. It seeks their benefit before your own. It means denying yourself to ensure that their needs are met. Most often selflessness is seen—or not seen—in the little events of life. Seeking to live selflessly in your family will bring great blessing to you and to your children.

I was amazed at some of the times remembered by my children that I had acted selfishly. My question, When were you most angry with me? evoked a vivid memory for Matt.

> We were driving from Colorado Springs to Nyack, and we were in Jersey somewhere. I was following you in the car with Brian and you were in the car ahead with Mom. I had to go to the bathroom, but you would not stop. I kept flashing the lights, pointing over to the side of the road, and honking, and I have never hurt so bad as I did that day. When we finally stopped, after I went my kidneys just kept aching, and that was the time I was most angry at you.

I had not even remembered the incident, even though it had occurred only two years before I interviewed Matt. For him it was a major episode because of my obstinate self-centeredness. I don't blame him for getting angry at me. I'm glad that is not Matt's only memory; on another occasion he saw me make a huge sacrifice for Betzi. It had to do with giving up Chelsia, our spunky, eight-year-old foster child. What to do about Chelsia when we were moving from Pennsylvania to Colorado was probably the toughest decision our family has faced. We all loved her, but Betzi and Brian had the roughest time with her unpredictability and need for attention. Betzi had also just finished her bachelor's degree and at age forty-three was more than ready to begin a new career. When I asked, What decisions disappointed you most? Matt replied:

> Getting rid of Chelsia, but that wasn't so much your choice. I think you made the right choice in sticking by Mom; one thing I did enjoy about that choice—you said that any one of us could probably argue Mom into accepting her, taking her with us, but in the long run that wouldn't really help anyone because you could change her mind for a while, maybe forever, but if this is a gut reaction, a gut feeling, then that's not something you want to change.

Although the decision not to take Chelsia with us was painful for Matt and me, he respected me for making a selfless decision.

Demonstrating selflessness around the house seems to be a big thing to children. Chris and Matt showed their sensitivity to this, and my need to improve, when I asked, How can I be a better dad? Chris said, "Maybe help out around the house more often. But that makes you a better husband more than a better dad." Matt commented, "There are always things to suggest—help out around the house more, stuff like that."

The second clause of this Daditude may seem simplistic, but as I have observed dads, I have found it to be true: Blessed are dads who are selfless, for they just make good dads.

A DADSHIP DARE

Review your disciplining practices and compare them with some of the advice given in this chapter. Do you punish or discipline? Are you emotionally closer to your kids afterward, or more distant?

7

Train a Child

One of the biggest mistakes new parents make is assuming there is a right way to raise children. From Dr. Spock to Dr. Dobson, the last two generations have had a plethora of voices advising us. Some of their principles may apply in most cases, but Solomon, who also had a lot of wise, fatherly advice, gave us the most important concept for child rearing: "Train a child in the way he should go, and when he is old he will not turn from it" (Prov. 22:6).

The genius of this proverb is its recognition of the individuality of each child. Solomon might have said, "Train children in the way they should go," implying a universal strategy for child raising, but he did not. God delights in variety. And children provide a staggering variety, even within one family.

"Glenn Clark, one of the great teachers on the life of prayer in the past generation, said that every child comes into the world with 'sealed orders.' Every human being has a unique destiny to fulfill."[1]

Dadship and Discipleship

Before we become parents many of us expect that there's a certain technique to raising kids, a formula or recipe. We also expect that kids are basically all the same. About two months after the second child is born we lose those false notions. Kids aren't like cars with different features that all run mostly the same. They are more like the contents of the Schroeder miscellaneous closet. Because we have moved often, it seems we never quite get completely settled. So we have a place where anything goes. Photo albums, tennis rackets, ice cream makers, Pictionary, a huge kettle, trays, dog food, folding chairs, a lantern, windshield washer fluid, recipe books, and a motorcycle helmet are a few of the items currently in our miscellaneous closet.

None of these things have much in common with the rest, except that we obviously value all of them or we wouldn't have hauled them around so often. So it is with our kids. There may be some similarities, but most parents are startled by the extreme differences among their children. Our three are no exception. The genetic pool surely must be vast. Chris is out-front, self-assured, direct, aggressive, and usually cheerful. Matt is creative, humorous, laid-back, socially popular, and intellectual. Brian is analytic, cautious, methodical, disciplined, and helpful.

Chris loves classical music; Matt went through an oldies phase and then into pop rock; Brian is eclectic—our five-carriage CD player might have hymns, jazz, Christian rock, classical, and rag at the same time when Brian is at the controls. All three kids love sports but approach them differently. Chris is extremely competitive, injury prone, and did well in team sports. Matt is reckless, less coordinated, but never gets hurt. He enjoyed team sports, but wasn't a star. Brian has the best athletic mechanics, but does not tolerate pain well. He prefers spontaneous neighborhood sports to organized team sports. In skiing, Chris wants to be the first down the slope; Matt wants to ski by the edge, veer into the woods, and hit all the jumps; Brian wants to find new trails and beautiful scenes and is quickest to find the hot chocolate.

The crazy thing is that they like each other intensely as friends, although it has not always been so. Chris and Matt, being closer in age, excluded Brian from their most confidential fellowship until his midadolescence. Chris was first to accept him; Matt took a bit longer. I think kids often feel jealous about the positive attributes of their siblings. How important it is to affirm their individual strengths!

Unique Training

Training takes place in the military, athletics, the arts, education, and industry. A more experienced, authoritative person takes time and effort to communicate ways for the trainee to meet new expectations. The relationship between the trainer and the trainee is vitally important. They must respect each other and agree to cooperate. Usually, younger children are eager to please their parents, so if teaching can begin early, the chances for training continuing into the adolescent years are increased.

Family counselor Larry Christenson observes,

> Nothing is so helpful in the training of a child as the opportunity for significant work. One of the real problems connected with the urbanization of our culture is that our children have fewer work opportunities. Nevertheless, parents must see to it that their children develop good work habits. Work around the house must be given over to the children as soon as they are able to handle it.[2]

Training children is different from every other kind of training in one important regard. In every other training experience, the focus is on getting the trainee to do something better, whether it is hitting a baseball, firing a rifle, or making a speech. Training children ought to be focused on *being,* rather than on *doing.* If our children get the impression that we are training them for our own advantage, early on they will learn to despise the instruction, sensing that we are using them as involuntary labor. The only legitimate focus for training children is character development. When your son understands that clearing the table after dinner is his chore because he must learn to handle responsibility in the home so he can have a successful life later on, he may more readily cooperate. Sadly, many parents do not discuss the rationale behind the training, which breeds contempt in their children for the least assignment.

In disciplining our children, Betzi and I soon learned what worked and what didn't for each of them. And they responded differently to different kinds of discipline during different phases of their growth. The one-size-fits-all approach to child raising is not only a sure way to alienate your children from you and from their best future, it also is a violation of Scripture. The uniqueness of every individual needs to be understood, respected, appreciated, and catered to.

Chris responded best to firm words. Her respect for my authority was so deep that a frown could reroute her intentions. Spanking Chris was like a violation of her personhood; it was usually far more than she needed because she wanted to be obedient and trustworthy. Matt was different. He didn't seem to hear verbal instructions very well. Betzi's wooden spoon was sometimes needed to get his attention and compliance. Brian needed logic. He had to understand why what he did was wrong or why what we wanted was reasonable. Like Chris, avoiding a spanking was always high in his priorities.

Parents need to learn very early in a child's life how best to apply discipline to that particular child. Because discipline should always restore and instruct, rather than punish, every act of discipline should be an act of love. So it is important to know how best to love each child, even while disciplining.

One way the differences between children in a family have been analyzed is by noting their birth order. Interesting studies have shown some generalizations about the oldest, the second oldest, and so on, down to the youngest. Gender plays a factor, too. Our three may be fairly typical. I asked them to reflect on the impact of their particular places in the family.

CHRIS: I'm supposed to be the forerunner, and the younger ones seem to have it easier. I've been looked at as more of a leader than the other two, and I think that I am. I'm also more responsible because I'm the oldest. Also I tend to respond to guilt more. I have to do this or that, or I'll feel guilty for not being responsible. As the oldest and the only girl, I have a very unique position in our family. Sometimes I can get away with doing things the boys can't. And at other times I have to take on more than they do.

MATT: I'm more gregarious than the other two, somehow, and I think that has something to do with being the middle child. I think I'm more independent, and although I'm very loved, I'm not as tied to the family as Chris and Brian are. I don't even remember being home my last year of high school, so it wasn't a hard transition to live on my own in Pennsylvania when you moved out to Colorado. It wasn't hard at all to see you guys leave.

And then college came right after that. I was never much of a homebody, whereas Chris and Brian were more so. You could relate better to me because, like you, I was the middle child. We've gone through some of the same things. Whenever I'm doing something dangerous, I know you guys aren't worrying, or whenever I'm just out somewhere, other kids would have to call their parents, but it made me more confident and competent that you didn't worry.

BRIAN: It was very difficult having Chelsia around because I wasn't used to having someone younger than me there. Just dealing with her was very difficult. Also you had to deal with me and my rivalry with Matthew. You knew how to handle that.

Unique Spiritual Nurture

Another way children display God's variety is in how they are wired spiritually. Just as each child is born with physical and mental properties that are unique, so each comes with a certain spiritual DNA that determines much about his or her religious life. Some children very early display a genuine sensitivity to God and an eagerness to please him. We think that this is the way it ought to be with all children, and if it is not so with our child, we have done something wrong. The pace a child develops spiritual instincts cannot be controlled by parents or anyone else. You cannot force-feed children what their appetites are not yet ready to receive. Throughout my childhood, I dreaded meals when the menu was either Chinese food or pizza. Today, I think all by myself I could keep Pizza Hut and Wong's profitable. But I didn't learn to like those foods by being forced to eat them.

Does this imply indulging a child's laziness or disinterest in the things of God? Not at all. I do not recommend the popular idea of allowing children to be architects of their own spiritual designs. In no other area of human life do we encourage children to act as though civilization has no wisdom or experience to benefit them. We expect them to take advantage of the learning of the past. But many parents think of themselves as enlightened when they neglect teaching values, religion, and spirituality to their children, allowing them to "look into it when they are ready."

I suggest that parents, dads especially, be sensitive to the spiritual makeup of their individual children. For example, Brian, whose "love language" requires spending significant time together, valued my efforts to meet weekly with him in a structured approach to devotional and discipleship growth. Saturday mornings we would go to McDonald's for breakfast and discuss his week's study of the book we were using. When I asked, What was the most important discussion we have had? he answered, "I would say the *Solid Ground* book that we discussed on Saturday mornings, although I don't remember individual questions. That book helped me as I was growing up, helped me to keep my life on line with God, and gave me a lot of basic ideas of how to keep growing."

Matt, on the other hand, valued his freedom; he did not want spiritual input in such a direct way. When he was a sophomore in high school, Matt's youth sponsor developed a program of devotions that all the members of the youth group were expected to observe. Matt didn't like the legalism of it and sought my counsel. I never knew the depth of his feelings until I asked him, What have been your biggest surprises from me? His reply: "One time my youth director was trying to force me to read the Bible and I didn't want to. You said, 'No, he shouldn't read the Bible until he wants to.' I don't know if you ever regret saying that, but I've always thought that was the best thing, and I guess that really surprised me."

I offer these illustrations not as evidence that I did the right thing for each of my children—the jury is still out—but to demonstrate how opposite the expectations and preferences may be in children from the same family. If all people were wired the same spiritually, there would not be such a wide and rich spectrum of Christian groups. Some offer a structured, liturgical approach to worship, while others have a wide-open body life fellowship. If whole denominations have such diversity, is it not because individuals exhibit such differences?

Unique Love Languages

My first venture into public ministry was as a youth pastor. After dropping out of seminary and being in business for three years, I was surprised when Betzi and I were asked to come to a church that had a dynamic youth ministry run by two effective but weary parents. We knew we were called to that ministry by the Lord, and we had a little confidence from our few years as youth sponsors, but moving to a new part of the country and being thrown to fifty teenagers was a bit daunting. I'd never intended to be a youth pastor and had not read one book about it. Noticing how effective and well liked the two parents were, I asked them, "What do you think we need to do to run a successful youth program?" I expected answers about programs and activities like concerts, retreats, and Bible studies. The three-word answer, "Just love 'em" was the most profound and effective advice I could have been given.

The power of unconditional love is awesome. Kids can overlook a lot of inadequacies if they know you love them, really love them. Maybe you have heard the idea of different "love languages." All of us have a preferred love language. For some people that language is verbal—they need to hear "I love you" and to be told why you love them. Others would say, "Say it with gifts." Some need and want a lot of physical closeness and tenderness, while still others prefer to be served in practical ways. Another language of love is time; some people know they are loved when the one they love is willing to spend a lot of time with them.

These are all legitimate love languages, and the important thing for us to know is how we can best show love to the ones we love. Genuine, biblical love is eager to know and meet the love needs of the other person. Children and young people have preferred love languages, just as adults do. Two adolescent nephews whose parents are divorced and who rarely see their dad are of great concern to me. The oldest is very active and physical. The best way I can meet his love need is be active with him in sports. The younger one wants to be with me no matter what we do; he needs my time and attention in conversation.

Discerning someone's love language is not difficult. Just observe how he or she shows love. Most people show love the way they want to receive it. Betzi is forever meeting my practical needs, even small needs I don't know I have. For example, when I return from a trip exhausted, she is quick to unpack my suitcase. Or when I have been ministering publicly, she knows I need private space and time, and she will ensure that I get them. That tells me that meeting practical needs is her love language, and if I am to love her best, I need to meet her practical needs. Watching your kids express love will tell you how they want to be loved.

I asked Chris, Matt, and Brian what were the favorite gifts we have given them. Their answers reveal a lot about their love languages.

CHRIS: Going to see *Phantom of the Opera* was a very special gift, and also my Bible; I have had it since '88 and still use it on a regular basis. Mom especially likes to buy things for me and I feel you have provided a lot of necessities and non-necessities throughout my life.

MATT: You and Mom gave me an antique gun, 1908 or 1906, from your grandfather. That was special. When I was in the hospital over my birthday, you guys brought in this huge, motorized, electric car set, as wide as the bed. Your father's Bible after he died. As much as I can, I really do appreciate that.

BRIAN: The bike for Christmas in New Jersey. A room of my own in New Hampshire and Pennsylvania because you made both rooms yourself, totally changing them from attics.

For Chris, family time together doing something she enjoyed was first on her list. Matt's best loved gifts were symbolic of his connection to our family line. Brian appreciated the personal effort I expended to provide private rooms for him in two houses.

The main point here, of course, is knowing the most appropriate ways to express love to each child. We sometimes try to force a love language on our children, which confuses them. One of the grievances my mother had, at times, against my dad was his not taking time to show me how to use construction tools. She thought it would be good for him to spend time with me as he built our cabin. On my behalf she would appeal to him, but without success. Dad worked fast and furiously and couldn't be bothered to slow down. The strange thing was I didn't want to help him. I was into baseball and BB guns, not hammers and saws. What my mom thought would have been a treat for me would have seemed like punishment.

What I remember from boyhood days that made me feel closest to my dad were the haircuts he gave me. Every few weeks, down in the basement we would go with his shoe box of haircutting tools. I'd climb the three-step stool, sit up high with the dish towel draped around me, and enjoy my dad's closeness. After the towel came off and before I got off the stool, I would always look for a few of my stray hairs on my dad's neck or on his shoulder under his T-shirt, and with great delight, I would pull them off. It wasn't Dad's time I needed as much as the physical closeness. And I think he knew that.

Unique Spiritual Exercises

Some of the funniest scenes in the home of any Christian family occur when the children are young and the parents are trying to have family devotions. The eleven-year-old may really be into it, listening to the story, answering questions, and trying to memorize the verse. The eight-year-old is fidgeting, looking over his shoulder out the window to see if the other guys are playing ball yet. The baby is anointing her head with mashed potatoes and gravy. Dad pretends none of this is happening and forges on with the reading; Mom attempts to show interest in what he is saying, while the phone rings and the dog barks.

What's a family to do? From the pulpit and in magazines we are assured that the destiny of our family depends directly on this daily family devotional time. One might think all preachers and writers are single! Put a mashed-potatoed two-year-old next to the pulpit Sunday morning and see how well the pastor does.

We need to relax and be normal about communicating spiritual lessons to our kids. If family devotions work, great! But I'm not sure God requires such formality in the home. Another scaled-down church service every day may be tolerated by extremely compliant children, but other ways of bringing up children in the teaching and instruction of the Lord may be more effective. Sometimes we institutionalize religious practices and demand conformity as an evidence of true piety. For example, although I think it is a good practice to offer a prayer of thanks before each meal, maybe that habit becomes mere ritual without meaning if we do not consciously focus on the content of the prayer.

One time I visited a family who had just started coming to our church. The husband-father was a new Christian of Jewish heritage. His wife was raised as a Baptist and knew all the "Christian rules" but out of consideration for her husband didn't insist upon observing them. Soon after his con-

Our children will be more attracted to the Christ met in the everyday events of life than to a Christ force-fed down their throats like some bitter medicine.

version, Ken learned that Christians say grace to thank God for the food. The evening I visited them, Ken and Nancy were just returning from the grocery store. After bringing in all the bags and placing them on the counter, Ken turned to me and said, "Pastor, would you like to join us in thanking the Lord for the food?" He then proceeded to offer the most beautiful, sincere prayer of thanks for food that I have ever heard.

It was like a prayer of dedication. Later I asked Nancy about this unusual practice and learned that they did not say grace at mealtimes, but only when they bought the groceries. This was simply Ken's idea of how best to express thanks to God.

Freedom to pursue authentic spiritual exercises can result in some wonderful, fresh activities. Our children will be more attracted to the Christ met in the everyday events of life than to a Christ force-fed down their throats like some bitter medicine. Experiencing God ought to be fun and exhilarating for children and adults. There should be pleasure, not pain, in his presence. Be creative. Find fun and real ways to teach your kids to love God as you do. Don't let anyone enslave you to a ritual that no one enjoys. Lasting lessons are best learned when the process is enjoyable, even fun.

A DADSHIP DARE

Have you discovered the love language of each of your children? How does or doesn't your approach to training them square with their need to experience your love in a particular way?

8

The Family That Plays Together Stays Together

Play makes all other parenting tasks effective and bearable. Playing with your children from their earliest months through their adolescence may well be the difference between raising rebels or disciples. If you want to build a healthy rapport with your kids, playing is not optional. If you were to interview parents in family therapy because of the rebellion of their children, my hunch is that you would find they never had time to play with their kids. The family that plays together stays together. Conversely, the family that does not play together does not stay together.

Having fun can be downright hard work for some of us. Many people, raised with the good old Protestant work ethic, honestly believe that fun is something they have to leave behind on their way to adulthood, like comic books and sweetened cereals. Many adults—many men—think play is synonymous with childishness. After all, real men live in a serious world with real problems, not in the fictitious world of childish make-believe. Fun is restricted to entertainment and is justified only because it may be viewed as relaxation in preparation for more productivity.

Even when men do play, we tend to turn it into something that produces stress. Gordon Dahl, author of *Work, Play, and Worship,* says we tend to worship our work, work at our play, and play at our worship. Surely there is a legitimate kind of adult play, activity to keep us healthy physically and mentally. Too often, however, parents—dads—exhaust themselves by worshipping their work and then working at their play. They have few resources left for playing at home. A four-hour golf outing or a few vigorous racquetball games are good tonic for the soul, but not at the expense of important time with the kids.

Family play is decreasing as personal play increases. Many families in the 1940s and 1950s considered Friday night *family night,* a term I haven't heard for a long time. Family night has gone the way of the old Burma Shave signs, and maybe for a related reason—technoprogress, or in this case, tech-noprogress. The sudsy, foamy shaving lather has been replaced by the ever more convenient and comfortable electric razor. The fun, touchy-feely family night has been deleted by that other electronic marvel, the tube. Family fun in front of the tube is even passé because there are few programs desirable or suitable for the entire family, and now most American families have multiple TV sets, so we can watch individually our choices of cable options. Soon our personal computers will double as our personal TVs, ala CD ROM. The Internet is already becoming the new playground for adults and kids, so we see more people now surfing the net contacting strangers instead of relating face-to-face with their own family members.

Is individualization of activities evil? No, not evil, but bad for the family. Hunting and agrarian cultures required domestic cooperation for survival. A by-product of times in the forests and fields was bonding between dads and children. So many insignificant learning experiences etched wonderful memories in these children: how to cross a stream, how to get past a barbed wire fence without getting stuck, how to milk a cow, how to use quack grass as a whistle, how to build a campfire, how to use a knife and an ax, how to walk quietly, and—most importantly—how to imitate a caring dad. Such were the benefits of more primitive days for many children.

The advances of first, industrialization and now, computerization have made us a more productive and proficient society. But these advances have not improved family quality. The greater complexity and danger of machinery prohibit children from participating with Dad or Mom at work. And because work is now a place where Dad and Mom go, instead of something they do at home, children do not even get to see what their parents do, let alone to help them.

Principles of Play

On the family level, play is sharing activities that the children have chosen. Kids are pros at play. Playing is as natural to them as eating and breathing. Young offspring in the animal kingdom are fascinated with experimentation, competition, and physical accomplishment. Human children have the same fascinations and add mental accomplishments and social activities. There is no end to the inventiveness of children for finding ways to have fun. For kids, having fun is the goal of playing.

Let children choose activities for family times. We may be bored by a game they love, but if our goal is to bond more deeply with the kids, they must be convinced that we are giving ourselves without condition to them. In fact, I am convinced that kids know what bores us and purposely choose those activities to test how sincere we are in wanting to have fun on their terms. I taught my ten-year-old nephew to play

Dadship and Discipleship

Acquire last year when we went on a weekend retreat together. The game takes about two hours to complete and isn't particularly fun with less than three people. During that weekend, when I had expected to teach him lots of interesting things about the woods, maybe even track a deer in the shallow snow, instead, we played eight games of Acquire. He calls it To Get because that is how I defined *acquire* to him. The first thing Aaron wants to do when he comes to our house now is play To Get. It's one way he knows he will capture my undivided attention.

I think kids' play has been designed to humble adults. Until our children reach double digits in age, we can be assured that most of our time playing with them will be spent on the floor. The floor is a great place to keep things in perspective. It brings us down to their level, humbles us because of the discomfort it causes us, and strips us of all adult power advantage. Maybe playing on the floor is one of those child-like things God loves, since we know he loves humility.

Playing with children provides great opportunities to teach them. And kids won't resist fun instruction if we handle the situation correctly. Dr. Frank Cheavens cautions:

> If you are trying to teach your child anything and find that you are becoming too tense about the child's failure or success, stop for a while and come back to it later when you're not so tense. It's rather hard for some parents to teach their children without becoming irritated by failures. Children sense that irritation and it gives them a feeling of failing not only at the task but as a person in the eyes of their parents.[1]

Keeping the children in control of the play is vital. I'm always tempted to raise the level of play, make it more challenging, more sophisticated, more productive. Brian has always had a great throwing arm. We enjoyed playing catch until I began to exploit his gift. I began to convince Brian that he could be an excellent Little League pitcher. From that point on, our games of catch took on a new purpose, one that Brian didn't relish. I set up a home plate and pitcher's mound, taught him how to wind up and deliver, and began to call balls and strikes. End of play for Brian. I was no longer Dad playing catch, but an umpire judging his performance.

Is it wrong to encourage your son or your daughter to excel in sports? Not if that is what the child truly wants. But I suspect most children prefer to play with Dad than with an umpire. The stories of child athletes coerced by dominant fathers ought to caution us. Young tennis stars burn out before reaching the age of twenty; boys become football players destined for glory before they need to wear jock straps; prepuberty gymnasts take their schooling on the road and study on the run so they can compete. Behind this glorified child slavery is usually a dad or mom who is compulsive about pushing the child into stardom. Sometimes their motives are unabashedly selfish—financial gain, fulfillment of their own unrealized goals, or fame.

Kids don't need adults in order to play. They are experts at it and can usually find other kids to enjoy. When they give us the opportunity to enter their world of play, we should understand that we are guests and treat the occasion as a privilege. Polite guests do not tell the host what to do or try to outshine the host. One of the most important purposes of playing with your children is helping them gain a healthy perspective on competition—which you can do only if *you* have a healthy perspective on competition. For me, this was a problem, having been raised with the Vince Lombardi credo, "Winning isn't everything; it's the only thing." Should I let my kids win? What a dilemma! Is it better to let them win to build their self-esteem and confidence, or to be honest and beat them every time until they win legitimately? In games of luck they will win their share, but adults usually have an advantage in games requiring skill.

I don't have an answer to this dilemma except to suggest that plenty of luck games be played in the early days and that you keep in mind the goal of playing is not to impress your kids with your abilities but to bond more deeply with them. And not all playing requires competition. Creative activities that require cooperation will provide some of the best fun times for you and the kids. In these activities it's important to find the right balance between helping and taking charge. I always wanted to take over a project to make sure it was done right. A simple axiom may help: The goal isn't to get the project done right, but to get the kids done right. Playing with the kids may quickly put the spotlight on our own immaturity. Maybe we have as much to learn as they!

Here are five more prime reasons you must make playing with your children a high priority.

Play to Communicate

Playing together is the only way we can achieve level Child to Child communication and relationship. In his popular book on transactional analysis, Thomas Harris shows that each of us has P-A-C relationships, that is, we relate as Parent, Adult, and Child in different situations and with different people. In most of our encounters with our children we relate as Parent to Child, and they respond as Child to Parent. Because the lines don't cross, effective communication can occur. However, only one kind of communication occurs, namely, authoritative. Whether we are issuing orders at the moment or not, the Child is very alert to the Parent's superior position.[2]

Occasionally achieving Child to Child communication is very important to fostering a healthy, loving relationship. Children need to see us as big children in order to trust us fully. And the only way for that to occur is for us to play together. Children cannot come up to our level, at least not young children, to establish an Adult to Adult relationship. We must condescend to their level. I use the word *condescend* to draw an important analogy. The only way God the Father could communicate the depth of his love was by condescending to us in the incarnation of Jesus. He had to become our size, to sit on the floor, as it were, and play with us.

Another image is suggested by the apostle John when he writes that Jesus became flesh and "dwelt among us" (John 1:14 KJV). This phrase may be rendered "pitched his tent with us." Have you ever camped out with kids? Most kids I know think tents are mansions. They love pitching a tent and sleeping out. That's a good way to achieve a Child to Child relationship—together, on the same level lying on the ground, exposed to the same joys of discomfort, telling stories and giggling or screaming together, depending on the stories. Remember this: If communication is going to happen with your kids, you have to make it happen, even if it means pitching a tent, like Jesus did with us.

Play to Teach Values

Playing together is the best time for teaching key values. You say, "But won't teaching cause me to revert to the Parent role?" If that's your thought, congratulations. You are showing the sensitivity needed to be a good play partner. This is a right concern. Maybe the best time for teaching is not the moment when a game would be interrupted or when your child would be embarrassed in front of a friend. Some of the values you will want to teach your kids, however, can only surface during play times.

Fairness is a good example. All games have rules that curb individual freedom for the enjoyment of all. To some kids and to many adults, winning is more important than everyone's enjoyment, even if it means cheating. Games and projects provide opportunities to emphasize fairness and its corollary, sharing.

Teamwork is another value best taught by playing. The men's basketball team at our college has an outstanding slogan: Excellence begins with WE. These young men are learning the value of teamwork. Employers look for a cooperative spirit. Learning to work well with other people is one of the most important lessons in life. The best activities for teaching teamwork feature a common goal, like putting together a puzzle or playing a team sport like volleyball. In this day of spoiled and pampered athletes, it is refreshing and rare to see a humble star who does not celebrate his or her own achievement in a team sport. When Matt played midget football, the only award I wished for him, and one he earned, was the Coach's Award, for the best team player.

Creativity is also best communicated during play times, sometimes unexpectedly. Dr. Cheavens writes,

> I observed a young father tooling leather. His three-year-old daughter was watching. After she had carefully observed the process, she sat down with the leather-working tools and pounded out a truly beautiful design on a small piece of leather. Her father was not afraid to let her use the tools and didn't discourage her because she was too small. This is a good example of how creativity starts.[3]

Perhaps the primary factor in developing creativity is an atmosphere of freedom, where achievement is not as important as effort. Maslow has shown that the most creative people have been raised in environments where experimentation was encouraged and failure not discouraged.[4] When we are playing with our kids, it is important to keep the stakes low.

Developing concentration skills is another benefit of playing with your children—theirs and yours! Children have built-in boredom barometers; they will detect your disinterest quickly. Playing a game while you talk on the phone, for example, sends a sorry message to your child. It says, I'm with you out of obligation, not because I want to be.

Many games and projects require sustained effort, and while some children have chemically caused attention deficit disorders (ADD), many people lack the discipline to concentrate simply because as children they never learned to sit patiently to complete a project. When they see us modeling concentration and patience, children begin to build these values into their lives.

How to be good sports can be taught as you play with your children. A person's character is revealed by the way he or she handles both victory and defeat. Winning well requires humility and respect for the opponent; losing well requires self-control and magnanimity. Our culture surely is not an ally in teaching these virtues. Quotes like the one attributed to Leo Durocher, former manager of the Dodgers—"Good losers lose"—don't help. The truth is many good losers win on the court or field, and all good losers win in character competition. As you play with your kids, teach them to be good winners and good losers. You may well be the only one who does.

Play to Spend Quality and Quantity Time Together

Playing with your children provides both quality and quantity of time together. In previous centuries the distinction between quantity and quality of time with children was not an issue. A father was home or near home most of the time. The interaction was frequent and deep. Dads might not have even understood the concept of quality time—an idea of rather recent invention used most frequently to excuse abusive absence.

We aren't all doting dads who go to every ball game or recital. Not all of us have hours each day to play with our kids. Not many of us put them to bed, reading stories and praying with them. However, it is not the quantity of time but the quality of dad that matters. Quality of time or quantity of time without a quality dad just won't cut it with the kids. By quality I'm talking about character. The character qualities that make biblical disciples make the best dads.

95

Dadship and Discipleship

Providing adequate quality and quantity of time by playing is probably the most important thing a dad can do to raise healthy children. Children instinctively yearn for Dad's attention. Clyde Narramore illustrates this with two short stories.

> I'll always remember the time I was giving an individual intelligence test to a little boy in the first grade. After I had worked with him for a little while he looked up and said, "You know what?"
> "No, what?"
> "My daddy loves me."
> "How can you tell?"
> "Because"—a big grin spread over his face—"Because he plays with me."
>
> Third-grader Ken was explaining to his uncle, "My friend Tommy can't catch a ball. He fumbles all the time. Know what I think, Uncle Bill?"
> "What, Ken?"
> "I think his daddy doesn't play with him like our daddy plays with Bruce and Kathy and me."[5]

Kids prize that time together with Dad for many reasons we may think are trivial. Sometimes a game gives them a chance to be on your side. Ever notice how all the kids want to be on Daddy's side? Playing together also gives them the opportunity to beat you, a great confidence booster. They also have your complete attention. And most importantly, when you play with your children they have the joy of having you on their turf. Whether you are in their rooms, their tents, their tree forts, their ball courts, or wherever, kids are honored and delighted to have you on their turf. Today their turf includes the personal computer, and dads need to spend time with their kids on that toy, too.

But the kids aren't the only ones who benefit from quality and quantity time together. You will get fresh glimpses into their characters and your own. You will also have an opportunity to model the character you want them to develop. Part of that is showing your humanness, availability, and approachability. And these play times will keep you young at heart. Finally, use these opportunities to show that being a Christian can be great fun. Christian parents who don't play are inadvertently sending a message to their kids: Faith is a grim, dreary way of life, and you must choose between Christ and fun. For a child, that's not even a choice. What a lousy message.

Play to Show Approval

Playing with your kids gives the opportunity to show them your approval. Young people are insecure. They get knocked around by bullies, ridiculed by their peers, punished by adults, and discouraged by their own childish inabilities.

Christian parents who don't play are inadvertently sending a message to their kids: Faith is a grim, dreary way of life, and you must choose between Christ and fun. For a child, that's not even a choice. What a lousy message.

Often their most in-depth interactions with Mom and Dad occur during discipline. They need spiritual and psychological refreshment. They need to be encouraged, affirmed, applauded, appreciated, and stroked. Did Janie beat you at Old Maid? "What a clever girl you are, Janie!" Did you and Joel put together a model airplane? "Joel, you sure are good with these tools, and how well you can concentrate!" Did Shawna skate around the rink without falling? "Shawna, I never knew you were such a good skater!" Did Miguel score on a new move to the basket? "Wow, Miguel, where did you get that move?"

Words of approval like these from Dad are priceless to a child. Nothing is more powerful for building strong self-esteem. On the other hand, criticism will tear down a child's sense of self-worth, so be sure to use the play times to show approval.

Play to Build Family Unity

Playing with your children builds family unity. Modern life has a million ways to tear apart a family, but where I see healthy families, whether Christian or non-Christian, I see parents playing with their kids. Our Christian faith is the foundation for building a strong family, but playing together is the mortar that holds the building together. Howard Hendricks says it this way:

> A young adult should be able to say, "Boy, I can still remember when we used to get together and play games. Pop would be lost in it. I used to think, there's my father, this great big leader, acting silly. It was wonderful! I knew he was for real." You see, that's what draws a family together. That's the stabilizing influence that keeps a kid from going off the deep end. Don't ever forget it, the fortification of family fellowship.[6]

A DADSHIP DARE

Just do it! Plan an event that will thoroughly delight your kid(s), and set a date and time to do it. Let nothing interfere.

9

Raising the X-Generation

Dadship is like men's fashion. There may be some changes from time to time, but the qualities that go into being a good dad remain the same from generation to generation. The Daditudes are the basic attire for effective dadship. Those qualities never go out of style.

Occasionally a new breakthrough in fabric or lifestyle requires a new kind of fashion even for men. Spandex and cycling came together to create a whole new fashion. It became fashionable to ride a bicycle and to wear Spandex shorts while doing so. A cultural shift—the exercise craze—required a fashion adjustment. It doesn't happen often, but it does happen.

Likewise with dadship. A megashift in our culture requires some additional dadship attire. The megashift is the arrival of the X-Generation, the daughters and sons of builder and baby-boomer parents. These young adults born between 1961 and 1981 experienced so many rapid cultural shifts in their formative years that their responses to the world around them are very different from any other generation.

Dadship and Discipleship

To use a metaphor, previous generations were like roadways getting smoother, straighter, and wider, changing from primitive walking paths to horse-and-buggy dirt roads to two-lane asphalt roadways to interstate highways. We boomers swerved off the smooth, straight highway of our culture, and now the X-Generation has hit a pothole and has been thrown into white-water rapids. Their experience of culture has been an unpredictable ride of the rapids.

Am I overstating it? Consider these words that are the rapids they must negotiate, words that have shaped them enormously: the pill, computerization, drug traffic, Madonna, multiethnicity, latch-key kids, legalized abortion, shopping malls, AIDS, education loans, MTV, gangs, low SATs, feminism, teen suicide, and so on. Most thirtysomethings and older have merely observed these phenomena happening to our culture. The X-Gen has been raised in this climate. These things haven't happened to their culture—they are their culture.

The literature about the X-Generation continues to grow, but if you want an informative and entertaining dose of X-Gen scoop, you'll find it in Neil Howe and Bill Strauss's *13th Gen*. From their book I have identified five areas of radical cultural shift that require special dadship strategies. You might wonder, Why bother? If the last of the X-Gen-ers were born in 1981, they'll soon be adults. It's too late to apply new dadship techniques, isn't it? Answer—No. One of the characteristics of the X-Gen is that they are slow bloomers. A hilarious cartoon in *13th Gen* shows a suburban house, the "Boomerang Motel." An X-Gen son is returning from college to this friendly environment featuring a Nintendo video arcade, Pop's Rent-a-Car (free gas), and Mom's Diner, ATM, and Laundromat ("We fold and iron—no extra charge"). Howe and Strauss note that among those who leave home with a high school diploma or higher, 40 percent—and well over half of the men—boomerang back to their parents' homes at least once. The opportunity for dadship influence may still be there, or it may return!

X-Gen Profile

Knowing that this two-decade generation has its own ethos and identity has not been a problem; knowing what to call it has. The 13-Gen terminology is preferred by Howe and Strauss (pp. 16–17), but X-Gen is probably better terminology for two reasons: (1) this generation doesn't want to be labeled, and *X* is as innocuous as any label can be, and (2) the X-Gen is often profiled for what it isn't, can't, hasn't, won't, and so forth. Shunning Howe and Strauss's label, let me still turn to them for the profile. X-Gen-ers are

> eighty million young men and women, ranging in age from 11 to 31. They make up the biggest generation in American history (yes, bigger than the Boom); the most diverse generation—ethnically, culturally, economically, and in family structure; the only generation born since the Civil War to come of age unlikely to match their parents' economic fortunes; and the only one born this century to grow up personifying (to others) not the advance, but the decline of their society's greatness. . . .
>
> News clips document a young-adult wasteland of academic non-performance, disease-ridden sex, date-rape trials, wilding, and hate crimes. Today's youngest sports figures often look to elders like American Gladiators, athletically proficient but uncerebral, uncivic, lacking nuance. To older eyes, the Neon Deions differ from the Namaths and Aarons partly in their size, speed, and muscularity, but also in their in-your-face slam dunks, end-zone boogies, and weak team loyalties.[1]

Howe and Strauss go on to profile them in polyglot American cities, as urban unmarried teen mothers and unconcerned teen fathers; in 'burb and town life, hangin' out with nondirected friends; in schools, seeking to get in and get out with the least amount of inconvenience and debt possible;

and in young adulthood, looking for jobs that provide maximum income, fun, and flexibility.

As the profile develops in the colorful language of *13th Gen,* we builder and boomer dads get more nervous about how to relate to these creatures. In some ways they seem extraterrestrial. How can we instill our values when they view our idealism as hypocritical? How can we influence their loyalties to social institutions like the church when they haven't

Raising the X-Generation must begin with character that transcends generational distance, character that earns respect and remedies some of the boomer-generation liabilities, character based on eternal principles found in the heart of the One Father.

been able to trust the way we have handled institutions like marriage? How can we help them gain financial responsibility when we have mortgaged their future? How can we talk with them about sexual and social ethics when we spawned the new morality of anything goes, leaving them with AIDS, illegitimacy, and divorce? How can we talk with them about God when so many religious heroes have fallen to lust and greed?

These questions call for a lot more than one chapter at the end of a book, but one of the things the X-Gen-ers appreciate is bottom-line simplicity. And although these questions are complex, the beginning of an answer lies in one word: *character.* Raising the X-Generation must begin with character that transcends generational distance, character that earns respect and remedies some of the boomer-generation liabilities, character based on eternal principles found in the heart of the One Father.

One-Parent Families

The X-Gen has grown up with the ravages of domestic experimentation, a euphemism for the anything-goes morality that has fragmented families at an unprecedented rate.

> According to one major survey of 1970s-era marital disruptions, only one-fifth of the children of divorce professed being happier afterward—versus four-fifths of the divorced parents. Half the kids of divorce recall having felt unwelcome in their new pieced-together families. At best, divorce brought kids complicated new relationships with moms, dads, and unfamiliar adults—and new time-consuming hassles shuttling back and forth between parents trying to schedule in a little "quality time" under awkward circumstances. At worst, divorce meant violent quarrels, split loyalties, estrangement from one parent (usually the father), maybe even a move away from one's house and friends.[2]

A 1988 U.S. Public Health Service survey showed less than 51 percent of fifteen- to seventeen-year-olds living with birth father and birth mother.[3] We don't need to rehearse divorce rates here. Howe and Strauss's chapters 7 and 8 portray vividly the toll of divorce on the X-Gen. The point is to deal with it. You may be a dad who doesn't know what to do with his visitation rights. Or you may know someone like that. Does your son or daughter really want to see you? What influence can you be now? Listen to this twenty-two-year-old son of a divorced father: "You don't understand. My stepfather could be Saint Benedict or Saint Francis. He could walk on water, and it would not change the hurt I feel about my dad."[4]

Children, young and old, want and need their dads. The quality, in addition to the Daditudes, that kids in one-parent families need in their dads most is availability. They need, more than anything, to be convinced that you prize them and want to be with them. Words will not work here. Any sentence that needs to have a *but* won't cut it, such as, "Honey, you know Daddy would like to come to your school play, but. . . ." All their lives these kids have lived with *buts,* which mean to them, "You are low priority." For divorced dads of X-Gen kids, character begins with availability.

Apathy, Cynicism, and Crime

The emotional abandonment that X-Gen-ers have suffered due to builder materialism and boomer narcissism has created in them a deep distrust of anything or anyone they cannot control. Their response to authority: apathy. Their response to progress: cynicism. Their response to boredom: crime. X-Gen-ers are likely to be totally disinterested in most anything outside the orb of their own lives. Their who-cares attitude applies to politics, international affairs, classical culture, history, ideologies, and education that doesn't readily translate into income. Having seen and heard about so many social breakdowns, X-Gen-ers have become cynical about progress, values, ideals, and the future. For alarming numbers of them the formula has become: *apathy + cynicism = crime.* Not respecting the rights and possessions of others, not having meaningful work to do nor being prepared for it, not being guided by any transcendent principles, and not fearing harsh punishment if they are caught, many X-Gen-ers resort to crime. Not all join gangs in "New Jack City," but many have learned the tricks of technotheft, date rape, or general wilding.

How can Christian dads respond to these antisocial behavior traits? A concept popularized in books during the 1970s and 1980s but not generally applied, *tough love* is, I think, the best response to the apathy, cynicism, and crime of X-Gen-ers. Tough love says (1) I care about you; (2) I stand for some important values you need to respect; (3) You are not going to live your life in such a destructive way. Will it work? Maybe not all the time. But it's still the right thing to do. Its best chance is if you can convince your children that you care. The cure for apathy is meaningful work. Tough love stops indulging X-Gen-ers and insists they get their bodies out of the house to find work. The cure for cynicism is achieving progress with integrity. Progress without integrity is easily seen for what it is—more exploitation—and X-Gen-ers have seen that in abundance. But progress with integrity earns respect and begins to unsnarl the cynicism many of them harbor. The cure to crime? Social theorists have debated this for centuries. No simplistic answer will do, nor will one be offered. But if your own son or daughter is engaging in criminal activity, tough love has to take a stand. Don't tolerate it.

Economy and Technology

Answering for X-Gen-ers, Joanne Gordon said, "Our answer to the famous question 'What do you want to be when you grow up?' is 'Employed.'"[5] X-Gen-ers know they face some grim economic realities. The previous two generations have lived like there's no tomorrow, and that's virtually how X-Gen-ers feel. We've left them with an astronomical national debt, unfunded but promised social programs, and a technologized work environment that employs electronic gadgetry rather than humans. Technology is not the only cause of the tight job market; downsizing (now called rightsizing), mergers, and immigration have also changed the employment landscape for X-Gen-ers. Those who have gotten on the crest of the computer wave, and they are many, are doing very well. Many have become millionaires overnight. The Atari and Nintendo kids, so adept at manipulating images on screens, kept their computer science profs on the edge of professional insecurity complexes. Indeed, the X-Gen-ers who won Desert Storm were basically using sophisticated Pac-Man and Space Invaders skills they had mastered a decade earlier.

However, the general economic bust and technology boom are likely to intensify the haves versus the have-nots problem in America. How can a disciple-dad encourage his X-Gen children to respond properly? Repent and rightsize. Most of us have contributed to the problem of the uncertain economic future our kids face. We have been unquenchable consumers; we have indulged our affluent appetites; we have allowed our politicians to build up an intolerable debt load. We need to repent—to admit our sin, to ask forgiveness from our kids, and to change our ways. We also need to rightsize; that is, now, while many of us are in our peak-income years, we need to invest in our values, putting our funds into missions, social work, the poor, the aged, the orphaned, or other human and Christian causes. Our kids need to see our treasures go where we say our hearts are.

Purposefully, I have not recommended giving X-Gen-ers more or helping them find work. They do not need to be indulged more or treated as adolescents. If anything, use your leverage to force them to be more responsible.

Education and Careers

The strongest critics of the X-Generation have named them the Dumb Generation.

> In particular, we hear, 13ers are DUMB. They can't find Chicago on a map. They don't know when the Civil War was fought. They watch too much TV, spend too much time shopping, seldom vote (and vote for shallow reasons when they do), cheat on tests, don't read newspapers, and care way too much about cars, clothes, shoes, and (especially) money.[6]

I am an educator, and I am greatly alarmed by this dumbing of America. Typical American high schoolers attend classes only three-fourths as many days as Japanese students attend and increasingly take fluff courses. We have a serious problem brewing. More and more X-Gen-ers are less and less qualified for meaningful careers. Indeed, the idea of a career rather than just a job is a luxury many X-Gen-ers refuse to entertain. Some will do very, very well, but most will merely settle for a job. Work will define a person far less, which may be good. Far too many people are what they do. And there is nothing wrong with work for its own sake and to earn a living. God never promised that every person will enjoy the work he or she is given. A dad can give his son or daughter honor for any honest job. Never denigrate blue- or brown-collar jobs. Do not ridicule your son for flipping burgers at Hardee's.

On the other hand, we can demonstrate some values that will help. My three children, who are X-Gen-ers, have grown up with a love for reading and education for its own sake. College was not just to get a job, but for personal growth in mind and spirit. Obviously, I am eager for them to have worthwhile careers that draw on their educations. I will also be interested to see whether they will be lifelong learners.

The attitude we dads should demonstrate in the face of this education and career cultural reality is midway between contentment and intensity. On the one hand, we should affirm any honest work our kids do and affirm them for being more than just what they do; that's the contentment side. On the other hand, we should encourage them to be all they can be in their career pursuit. Notice, I said encourage them, not pressure them. If your son or daughter tries hard to get into a chosen profession and it just doesn't happen, pressure or criticism from you is not needed. Keep encouraging your children about who they are right now and about what they can accomplish for God regardless of their careers.

Sex and Leisure Lifestyle

Now we come to a cultural reality that may be very difficult for Christian fathers to face. Attitudes and values concerning sexuality have changed in the past few decades as much as technology has changed. The X-Gen-ers have inherited the new morality from us, the peddlers of free love.

> The first 13ers entered puberty to the sound of Marvin Gaye humming "Let's Get It On," a time when adults of all ages were emitting erotic signals everywhere and proclaiming their panting obsession with S-E-X. At breakfast, 13er kids could never be sure what overnight companion a parent would bring to the table. At school, their sex education was both antiseptically clinical and unabashedly value-neutral. After school, empty houses provided them with handy trysting spots to test what they had learned. After dinner, pop music and TV programs kept saying "Do it! Do it! Do it! ('til you're satisfied)." Then, on weekends, movies showed them how to close the deal.[7]

We'd like to think that those changes have happened only out there in the world, not here in our Christian ghetto. That is not true, however. Every kid has a friend who has had an abortion, is "doing it," is gay, feasts on porn, or lives some kind of deviant lifestyle. Some Christian parents have kids who fall into those categories.

Nearly as annoying as the sex menu our children choose from is the dessert tray of assorted leisure-time activities. Leisure, for them, does not fill in the gaps; leisure is it—the mainstay, the thing worth living for. Maybe a more accurate word is *fun*. Everything needs to fit into fun. If the job can be fun, cool! If not, get out quick so we can find some fun. Matt's three criteria for his first job after college reflect this attitude. "It's gotta be with people my age, I don't have to dress up or work at a desk, and it's gotta be fun."

So how should dads engage these attitudes toward sex and fun that drench our X-Gen-er kids? For me the word is *patience;* patience, patience, patience. The prolonged adolescence will give way to maturity, and, hopefully, we'll live to see it. One thing I know—putting a heavy parental trip on my kids won't help at all. My authority is no match for their hormones, and my admonitions will never daunt their quest for unabated, entertaining fun. Ride with it! But model what you hope they will become.

My prayer is that, because of your outstanding discipleship and dadship, the X of X-Generation will become a χ, the Greek letter at the beginning of *Christos*. What a thrill to see a Christ-Generation!

Happy dadship, Disciple!

A DADSHIP DARE

Talk with your family about how today's economic bust and technological boom will affect your family. Are you ready for the X-Generation?

Notes

Chapter 3: The Fourth World

1. Mary Jo Kochakian, "Many Men Have No Model for Fatherhood," Review of *Man Enough,* by Frank Pittman, in *Rockland (New York) Journal News,* 6 December 1993, C3.

2. Ibid.

3. Ibid.

Chapter 4: The Paternal Umbilical Cord

1. Joyce Brothers, "Is He a Good Dad?" *Reader's Digest,* June 1995, 114–18.

2. Ibid., quoting Henry Biller, *The Father Factor.*

3. Ibid., quoting Phyllis Bronstein.

4. Jerry Johnston, *Inspire Your Kids to Greatness* (Carol Stream, Ill.: Zondervan, 1993), quoted in *Marriage Partner 2* (fall 1994): 71.

Chapter 6: Manly Meekness

1. John Calvin, cited in John R. W. Stott, *God's New Society* (Leicester, England: InterVarsity Press, 1979), 247.

Chapter 7: Train a Child

1. Larry Christenson, *The Christian Family* (Minneapolis: Bethany, 1970), 64, quoting Glenn Clark.

2. Ibid., 66.

Notes

Chapter 8: The Family That Plays Together Stays Together

1. Frank Cheavens, *Creative Parenthood* (Waco: Word, 1971), 82.

2. Thomas A. Harris, *I'm OK—You're OK* (New York: Harper & Row, 1967), 76.

3. Cheavens, *Creative Parenthood*, 103.

4. Abraham Maslow, *Toward a Psychology of Being* (Princeton, N.J.: P. Van Norstrand Co., 1962), 127–37.

5. Clyde M. Narramore, *How to Succeed in Family Living* (Glendale, Calif.: Regal, 1968), 73–74.

6. Howard Hendricks, *Heaven Help the Home!* (Wheaton: Victor, 1975), 100.

Chapter 9: Raising the X-Generation

1. Neil Howe and Bill Strauss, *Thirteenth Gen* (New York: Vintage Books, 1993), 7, 9.

2. Ibid., 60.

3. Ibid., 61.

4. Ibid., 62.

5. Ibid., 100.

6. Ibid., 18.

7. Ibid., 148.